FRED

Confessions of a Grumpy Farmer

The Life and Times of a
Bitter Old B*gger and How
He Got There

Contents

Author's note

Everything written here is true, but may not always be entirely factual. In some cases, I have compressed events; in others I have made two people into one in order to maintain their anonymity. In some instances, I have changed the names of individuals and places. I may have changed some identifying details.

This book is for Rachel.

The Setting

My strong morals held me back from writing this book for decades. My shame stopped me from revealing the extent of my regret and bitterness. I was too decent to write about the backwards people that had caused me so much menace in the past, and the nuisance of contemporary people with no common sense whatsoever, but the great differences between townspeople and country people continued to cause me nothing but pain, leading to the eventual writing of this book as life corroded and weakened my morals. I learned that such morals are barely recognised by anyone anyway and that shame is only a figment of the imagination. Standards have slipped… and me along with them. This should provide the curious reader with some devious amusement. After all, you must be aware of the rough to appreciate the smooth, and this is all about my rough. As you read on, you may just find that you can begin to appreciate your smooth a little bit more than you currently do.

Life for me began in the farming environment of Northern England. This was far from the quaint images bestowed upon us of farming life in the home counties of Southern England and the stereotypical farms depicted in radio plays and TV dramas. Swap the long dreamy summers for cold wet rainy and seemingly endless winters. Change the Somerset accent for a Yorkshire one. Change the polite and civilised characters for rude and ignorant ones. Then, introduce random urbanites at every turn who cannot understand anything connected to the countryside, mix them all up together, and you have the unique and tormenting little niche that I resided in.

Born in the 1960s, everything was rearwards compared to today. The abundant old farm buildings across the region were not yet converted into the luxury homes that are commonly seen nowadays. Intelligent and successful people now live in them, but back then, they were full of cows, pigs, sheep, hay, straw, and sh*t. Unusual people worked on those farms; they were strange characters, types that are no longer seen. Since those days, education and society have greatly improved and people with issues are identified and given assistance. As for the disparity between practical farmworkers and domesticated townspeople, it has always been there – and it has become worse. This sets the general scene of my vinegary experiences.

Admit it or not, we all take pleasure in reading about other people's awkward and unfortunate experiences. Those "thank-goodness-it-wasn't-me" stories of things that have happened to someone else rather than ourselves that leaves us feeling relieved. It may only have been something watched on television, but we still shudder to think. Shameful examples include TV documentaries uncovering the embarrassing habit of hoarding in which cameras take the viewer into a home filled to the roof with rubbish and unneeded items such as clothes, toys, hardware and everything else you can imagine, not to mention the disgusting toilets and unhygienic kitchens. A huge clean-up operation usually ensues, and the "star" of the show is filmed pleading to be able to hold on to their belongings. Then there are programmes such as "Neighbours from Hell", taking viewers into the thick of some very uncomfortable feuds, or "Can't Pay? We'll Take It Away", taking us into the world of High Court Warrants and forceful repossession of homes and contents. The "stars" of the latter are very often living beyond their means and not paying their bills, and while they're effectively being publicly humiliated, they seem to be unaware of it. There are always underlying issues causing these lifestyle choices and dramas; these might be mental issues, emotional distress, depression caused by a traumatic experience such as a death in the family, or a physical decline, and this raises a moral question – should such car crash epics be exploited for entertainment?

This book is about the strange people I have encountered and suffered throughout my life and the crackpot characters that I've now come to resent. It also serves to explain why so many of the old farmers you meet today are hard-faced and generally unpleasant. I have been plagued and tormented by problematic people that have caused me pain, anguish, and untold stress through the uncomfortable situations they have put me in. These people include the impossible characters that have been acquaintances and colleagues as well as the townspeople I've encountered wandering around in the countryside and typically found to be nothing short of weird.

I write about the past and not the present, and I write about real-life observations and experiences. Farming and its characters have now changed and evolved. However, if there are any readers considering getting involved in farming in some way, it may be advisable to read the entire contents of this book and take very careful consideration:

Do not marry into farming if you don't know anything about it.

Read this book before taking up employment on a farm or moving to a new house near to one.

Read this book if you are trying to understand a farmer's mind.

The gap of understanding between farmer-types and non-farmer-types has been a huge contributing factor to my negative experiences. The two worlds overlap, and this is where misunderstandings and incompatibility create agony. My deepest regret is that all the admirable qualities I possessed in the past left me vulnerable to the people I met. I was honest and extremely hard working. I was moral and forgiving. I was generous and enjoyed giving rather than receiving. My genuine modesty was self-destructive; I never thought I was better than anybody else and I never thought I was above any job. I was open-minded, and I instantly accepted people for what they were without question. This, as it transpired, was all counterproductive and benefited only the needy people I seemed to encounter regularly.

Endurance was the last of my super qualities, adding to the lethal combination of traits that set me up for the long haul. I never gave up. I persevered where others would have given up or changed course, and I stuck with things because I knew and believed that they could be done. I had the right attitude, but it was always for a lost cause. There were hundreds of times when walking away would have been the better option, but I stayed and persisted. I stuck with people, painstakingly overlooking their obvious faults. In hindsight, it was all in vain. I was a martyr. No one ever knew of the effort I put in, so it was wasted. I may as well have put my efforts into trying to teach Shakespeare to a pig.

Looking back, I am sure that if I'd utilised my qualities in the right circumstances, there would have been no telling what I might have achieved with my life. I might have been an accomplished doctor, a politician, or even a successful businessman. I was polite and considerate and think that perhaps I should have been a vicar. That would have suited me, but, as it was, I was in the wrong place – just no one ever told me. I was too modest to see my own qualities and I was too busy being far too accommodating to everyone and anyone in need of help.

Alas, all of this is what I used to be. I will now tell you what I am: a bitter and resentful, suspicious, untrusting, hateful old misfit. I feel robbed and cheated. I am now socially barren and have no interest in anything anymore. My working life has been hindered by people who were nothing but a burden, and the non-farming people that constantly asked me for favours caused nothing but misunderstandings whenever they came into the practical world.

Farming and its satellites have physically wrecked me, damaging my back and impeding my breathing, and taken away and wasted my potential. Imagine it as before and after photographs… I went in looking like a young Arnold Schwarzenegger with a halo above his head and I came out looking like a decrepit old man sucking on lemons. I do take offence when people refer to others as being bitter and twisted because take my word for it, if someone is bitter and twisted, they have undoubtedly endured terrible hardships to get there. They will have been overcome by misfortune, and they do not need insult added to their injuries.

As I reflect, I realise that had I been planted into an intelligent environment all those years ago, I would not have cause to write this book. My life would have been something different. Have you ever driven past a half derelict sh*thole of a farm, one that looks like God has forsaken it, especially on a cold, wet day when the rain is horizontal? There's usually a collection of unidentified farm machinery strewn around the place as though a tornado has passed through, and there's always a steaming manure heap obscuring any possible view from the dwelling. Deep tractor tyre ruts run through the muddy yard, along with vicious-looking barking dogs. The roofs of buildings are falling in and cats lurk in every cubbyhole and peer through smashed, dust-caked windows. If you have, you'll have experienced an unmistakable smell of the countryside in the air and no doubt thought to yourself, "Who the bloody hell lives there?"

Well, it could have been me.

I either lived there or worked there. You may have seen me as you passed by in your car; we may have shared a glance. That was me. However, it was not the environment that left me so traumatised, it was the people that came along with it. Funny folks seemed to gravitate towards the countryside, almost like it was some sort of haven for those with issues as it took them away from society. I worked with the lower-end farmers who were struggling to make a living. They were small, cutthroat businesses in which thrift had no shame. The cheapest of farm labourers were employed, and no money was wasted paying for intelligence or manners. There were only two essential qualities a farmworker needed: the first was the ability to turn up and the second was muscle. The ability to turn up was the stumbling block that ended the prospects of most participants.

The Farmworkers

Many ad hoc farmworker interviews concluded with, "Come at 4", by which the farmer meant 4 am the next day. No-shows were common – they had fallen at the first hurdle. Most had the sense not to bother showing face again, but they never had the decency to say they were not coming back. In fact, there was no need because they'd failed the test without even realising that it was a test. It always amazed me how desperate people could be for the chance of a new job, only to forget to set the alarm or just roll over in bed when it went off in the morning. The realisation of having missed hours of work when they finally awoke on what should have been their first day must have caused a degree of embarrassment.

Those who did not have the sense to not come back were the worst. Their dismissal could take a while, with the inevitable being prolonged by me, my own worst enemy. I would cover up and carry the workload so that their appalling lateness went mostly unnoticed. I had a heart back then, and I knew that sometimes a young family was anticipating the wage packet. I created a second chance for them, then a third and fourth. The ruinous timekeeping would go on and on. This was incredibly inconvenient, especially at the weekends or on bank holidays when plans would be agreed to aim for an early finish. It would all end in disappointment when the weak link would let the rest of us down. Occasionally, there would be double time on offer when a job had to be done urgently. This was generally tractor work in the fields, perhaps re-seeding a field before the rain came or mucking out sheds before the harvest time when the tractors would be needed elsewhere. The extra hours would be snapped up by these less than reliable characters time and again, it beggared belief that they'd willingly do all that overtime only to then lose regular time every single day. Eventually, my efforts were all in vain. I couldn't carry the dead weights forever and the farmer in charge would ultimately sack them. He probably knew from the start that I was carrying the can, and probably thought he'd just let me get on with it if I was stupid enough.

Many of my more successful former colleagues had failed in several vocations before arriving at the farm. I always found out the hard way why that was. Farming can be a refuge for crank individuals who have fallen out with everyone in every place they've ever been, generally because they are too pig-headed to think they could ever be wrong and thus are incapable of learning from their mistakes. The same routine would play out wherever they took up employment. In the beginning, everyone welcomes the new face, seeing a newcomer as someone with a clean ticket and maybe a new friend to be made. Then the socially naïve mistakes begin. Initially, these mistakes may be considered friendly cheek or banter and perhaps even found amusing by some, but, inevitably, someone will take offence.

Unaware of the social boundaries that are painfully obvious to everyone else, the boorish asking of personal questions eventually leads to discomfort among work colleagues. Embarrassing questions about personal finances, disturbing enquiries into directions to home addresses, and unabashed probing into whose car is who's in the car park all begin to raise eyebrows, and the prying indicates a problematic individual. People begin to wonder why these questions are being asked and why the asker wants to know.

The brazen comparison between themselves and their new colleagues demonstrates that they are far from open-minded and they do not respect diversity. There's something that doesn't sit right with them, a disparity between them and everyone else, and they seem compelled to weigh everybody up. Being at the receiving end of such scrutiny creates an uneasy feeling and warrants a few steps back. The process begins again on the next unsuspecting victim, then the next, until there are inevitable tensions. Soon, all staff become aware of the danger and distances are kept as everyone returns to work as before, the excitement of the new colleague's arrival well and truly over. For the soon-to-be farmworker, not being overly involved in other people's business, and being told a few home truths into the bargain, is more than they can cope with. Job hunting resumes as they search, once again, for a fresh start.

Social skills are learned skills for all of us and there's no shame in this learning process, but most of the farmworkers I encountered back then had a complete inability to progress into anything remotely representing normal. However, the short-lived bouts of employment all over the place would come to an end once they arrived at the farm. They had found their destiny. On the farm, there were few people to fall out with and wide-open spaces meant social distancing complimented social inadequacy. Animals became human substitutes, and as they would happily absorb all conversation without taking any offence, and all insults or abuse would go completely unnoticed, this was a relationship that could work.

The icing on the cake for these characters was me. I buffered all the socially awkward moments and intervened in disagreements, often using humour to dissolve situations. I took the leftover tasks that no-one else wanted to do and I picked up the undesirable shifts to accommodate everyone else. It became evident that everyone preferred working with me – I was a mug. Shift work requiring two people always included me, and this was simply because any other combination of staff wouldn't get on quite so well together. They were too much alike. I was always piggy in the middle. King of pigs. I was a friend to all, but, unbeknownst to me at the time, this was a dangerous situation to be in. Some of these individuals had never had a friend before. I was in danger of being stalked.

Bernard

His name was Bernard, and in many ways, he was the worst colleague I ever had. He was in his twenties, over six feet tall and overweight, he had wonky eyes, and wore typical 1980s-style large glasses, woolly hats and cardigans. He had worked all over the place, and now he was working with me. Having already mocked those who failed to show up for work in the morning, there now comes a flip side: complete and utter fruit loops have no issue with getting to work for four o'clock in the morning. They never fail to turn up. This gruesome hour of the morning is practically neither day nor night, and during the winter months, it feels like a wholly unnatural time to be awake, like a witching hour, yet this can suit the unsociable outcast who doesn't have much of a life. For anyone with a family at home, these early shifts can be unbearable. The comings and goings of family life, the associated outings and evening events to attend, and the occasional need to care for a poorly partner or child well into the night can be tough when you're facing an early start in the morning. Sleep deprivation takes its toll, and if you're feeling under the weather and just need an extra hour or two in bed – well, you can't.

There were plenty of occasions in my youth when I was the designated driver on a lads' nights out. Once they were drunk and out of control, it was like mission impossible trying to get them back in the car so that I could get them and myself home. No-one gave a toss that I had to go to work at stupid-o'clock in the morning, and I'd end up having to set my alarm to go off just two hours after getting to bed. I'd have to rip myself out from under the covers and go to meet Bernard – who had probably spent the whole evening waiting in his overalls.

Bernard was always there when I arrived. He would already have clocked in, but he would never have started doing anything. I think this was to make sure he didn't do any more than I did. His face would be burning red or sometimes even purple and he'd shout, "Come on! We have all these f***ing cows to milk." He seemed to work himself up in this way, anticipating the job rather than just getting on with it. We'd get started and he'd rein himself back into a moderate fluster. After all the screaming, I never did bother to tell him that we were both twenty minutes early anyway. This was a thing that Bernard did; he always came early. Why come earlier than 4 am? It was ridiculous, but I stupidly went along with Bernard's strange timekeeping when I worked with him; it kept him stable.

After hours of stressed panic and unnecessary screaming, Bernard would then be in a good mood at the end of the shift. He'd often invite me to join him at the café for breakfast. This never failed to stun me because during the entire shift he would be so aggravated, he gave the distinct impression that he wanted to be somewhere else, yet once finished, he seemed to have nowhere to go and then wanted to spend time with me. When Bernard worked early, he didn't come back to work the same day. This was fair enough. I, however, had to go back and milk the cows again with someone else, leaving me with only two or three hours to rest before the next shift started. I swear to this day that Bernard deliberately pestered me right up until the time I had to go back to work, just to ensure that I had no rest in between.

I eventually stopped going to the café because it was too far away, after travelling and waiting for the food to be cooked, it left me with no time to go home to sleep between shifts. This left Bernard at a loose end and he was no longer able to deprive me of my time out. One morning, after a particularly heated ordeal with Bernard, I told him that it was like looking after a toddler working with him. This was true. He was very needy and couldn't do anything on his own. He sought consultation on every minor issue, and by the time I had stopped what I was doing to deal with his queries, it would have been quicker to just do it myself. He was also very childish, grabbing at the newer equipment – the shiny hand tools rather than the tainted ones and the tractors with the marginally newer registration plates. It took me a while to notice, but when I did, it brought a smile to my face as I thought, "Little things and little minds."

Getting into my car and driving off our separate ways at the end of the morning brought me an almost overwhelming feeling of relief, but this feeling was not mutual. Imagine my horror as I arrived home to find Bernard's car parked up outside. He knew my family and my neighbours and had his face stuck in everywhere, so I could only assume it was none of my business who he was seeing or why he was there, he hadn't mentioned anything to me. I slipped in my door, made a cup of tea, and settled down to relax in front of the TV. Two sharp knocks at the door followed, and it sounded urgent. Before I could think of an escape plan, the door opened, and Bernard was in. "Are you in?" he said, acting as if he didn't know, then adding, "get the kettle on, I'll have a quick pot o tea wi yer," which made it sound like he might be in a rush. It was an awkward situation, but I tried to gloss over it as I always did. In the time it took me to make the tea, he'd parked himself in my chair with the remote control in his hand. "What's this yer watching?" he asked, instantly disapproving of the BBC news and switching channels to watch adverts. Conversation didn't flow naturally, but we discussed some farming issues and things of mutual interest such as pay rises and tax deductions, making it the closest to a normal conversation I'd ever had with him. I knew he was a character, so I was polite and courteous, and I didn't make a big deal of things.

Besides, I lived on my own at the time so there was no harm done, other than missing out on my rest again.

I thought no more about it until the next time I was working with Bernard. During that shift, a sense of dread came over me as I began to wonder if he might be planning to come back to my house to pester me all day again. I tried to prevent the situation from reoccurring by telling him that I felt exhausted and I was going to go straight to bed when we'd done. Once I got home, I made a cup of coffee and was settling into my comfy chair when to my horror, he appeared again. He made some excuse about coming to see a neighbour of mine, but they weren't home, and then proceeded to make himself a cup of tea and start arguing with the television. He knew I was irritated, but he didn't care. How ignorant to stay for no reason, knowing all the time that he was unwelcome. This had to stop.

He had me going in to work extra early to accommodate his bizarre timekeeping. He screamed all through the shift and made the job ten times harder than it needed to be. He scared the cows with all his noise, making them kick and sh*t everywhere, and to top it all off, he was going out of his way to ensure that I didn't get any rest, this made my second shift much harder. What's more, he'd stunk my house out and very nearly blocked the drains after using my toilet, then gone back to his own house to rest while I had to go back to work. With all of this said and done, he was also causing me embarrassment by coming around to my house. Surely the neighbours would be wondering what his business was with me.

Bernard was a burden and a prolific troublemaker. He would play farm staff off against one another, fanning the flames of any niggles that flared up between colleagues and constantly stirring up conversations about absent workers. Every effort to stop him coming back to my house had failed. Subtle hints fell on deaf ears, as did more direct statements such as informing him that I was busy or going somewhere. It was all I could do to stop myself from barrelling him with, "Do not come to my house, I do not want you there," even though I knew he already knew that. I began to delay my journey home by doing a bit of shopping on the way, hoping he'd think I wasn't coming home and go elsewhere. It didn't work. When I arrived back, he was just sitting there waiting in his car. In desperation, I eventually got around the situation by going to my sister's house for a rest, he didn't go barging in there. It was satisfying to think of him sitting there in his car wasting his time as I settled down to a well-deserved sleep. He was getting a taste of his own medicine.

To anyone less acquainted with these unusual types of characters, such shenanigans and escape measures may seem odd. Police interventions or injunctions might be considered a more normal approach, but Bernard was not normal. I don't know that he could help his behaviour, and I suppose I felt sorry for him. He still lived with his mother and had been forever single. I often wondered if there were people incarcerated in mental institutions who were less worthy of being there than Bernard would have been. It was just the way he was, and everybody knew it.

He once asked me to help him create an internet dating profile so that he could find himself a woman. He didn't have a computer and I knew this was going to be another ordeal, but I accepted the challenge. There was an unrealistic part of my imagination that managed to envisage Bernard settling down with a woman, and this would have been to everyone's benefit. It would calm him down, teach him things about life that he was unaware of, and I thought he might even lose the boiler suit and woolly hat, get a haircut, and upgrade to some conventional glasses. We made a profile stating his age, location, hobbies, and so on, and there was some initial interest from single women here and there. They all appeared normal enough to me, so I think the interest was mostly down to it being a new profile and they'd already exhausted all others on the site. A photograph was yet to be added. The messages kept coming and Bernard would pop round to my house to go through them all and send replies. He was happy and excited, almost a little too excited for comfort. His imagination was running riot and he was behaving like someone who'd already found love, although this was not actually with any individual. He even mentioned the possibility of having children, suggesting he might not have grasped the fact that only the most basic of dating preparations were being made. I tried to pour some cold water on his thoughts by telling him that the photographs could be fake and there may be all kinds of skeletons in the cupboards of these women. It then dawned on me that the same was true in reverse – Bernard himself was a complete horror show. Requests came in for a picture, so he reluctantly went to the bus station to get a passport photo. I don't think any other photos of him existed beyond those his mum had of him as a baby.

It's accepted that photo booths don't always capture the kindest of images, but as he handed me the picture, it took an Oscar-winning performance to obscure my fright. This was one of those unkind images. Bernard was ugly enough, but this picture made him look much worse than he did in person. He looked angry; he had probably lost patience with the photo machine whilst waiting for the flash and had no doubt begrudged having to put a couple of pounds into it. His skin was illuminated and the bright whiteness of it made his black stubble stand out. His thinning hair was flat, the woolly hat having been briefly removed, and the flash had somehow exaggerated the squint in his eyes. There was no smart shirt on show, just a stained T-shirt, and, unsurprisingly, all correspondence stopped as soon as the photo was uploaded. Some went so far as to block Bernard's profile to eliminate any possibility of further contact. He wasn't offended. In fact, he simply said, "Thank f**k for that," expressing his relief that it was over and that he wouldn't have the stress of having to meet any of them.

I tried to be a friend to Bernard, but he was incapable of friendship. He seemed compelled to extinguish any type of friendship that developed as if it was a threat of some sort. He would do this by pulling some unpleasant trick and then disappearing. I had seen him do this several times with others. He would develop routines of going to peoples homes on different days for meals. His appearances were often welcomed: he provided company for the extremely lonely, his ignorance was often seen as hilarious by naïve children, making them laugh, and he brought a wealth of information about other people's business for those who liked to gossip. His visits would be unplanned initially, then they'd slip into something regular enough to be considered a pleasant little social life – and then he'd just pull out. Without notice he'd stop coming, leaving the hosts with cooked food on the table. Bernard would be expected but he'd never appear again.

I think deep down he wanted to straighten his life out, and there must have been some deep-seated reasons for his conduct. He once told me that his mother had sent him to see a psychologist, telling me the story of how he fooled the doctor by giving fake or humorous answers to the questions that were asked. Perhaps he just couldn't be helped. Bernard was hard work, and I should have shunned him away and kept a distance. He stole my time and lowered the tone of everything, and all I got in return was pain and misery. In hindsight, I think the idea of an injunction wouldn't have been such a bad one after all.

George

Like myself at the time, George was another casual farmworker. He differed from Bernard in many ways, not least in that he was clean, well turned out, and looked like a normal person. He was very alert and physically fit, making him look younger than his years, and he was truly a hard worker. He would jump straight into the back-breaking jobs that usually saw others swiftly disappear, and my offers of help were neither here nor there as he never appeared to be overly concerned by the prospect of doing these tasks all by himself.

He was good. A little bit too good. He had to be busy all the time and if there was a spare ten minutes, he'd find some other job to do to fill in the gap. This could be a bit annoying, especially if it did need a second person, everyone other than George were more inclined to just take it easy for such a small amount of time. You could be forgiven for thinking he had shares in the place, and I eventually found out that George had been headhunted by the farmer. This was very impressive, and he must have been under surveillance and it had not gone unnoticed what a hard worker he was.

The first inkling I had of George potentially having issues was when I walked into a room and unintentionally startled him. He must have jumped a metre off the floor, knocking over a churn of milk in the process. I laughed heartily whilst George held his hand over his heart, eyes bulging and hyperventilating. A little later, it happened again when I spoke as I walked up behind him outdoors. The spanners he was carrying dropped to the floor as he shot into the air before he spun around to spit out, "You're going to give me a heart attack." I wasn't trying to jump him. This was something that just kept happening and things soon got a whole lot worse. Once the others noticed his nervous disposition, they were relentless in their mission to deliberately shock George at every opportunity.

He was highly strung and very panicky, and every conversation I had with George gravitated towards ailments, doctors, hospitals, and operations. There could be no doubt that he was a textbook hypochondriac. He almost always claimed to have an operation in the pipeline and was often in the process of waiting for a letter from the hospital. The first words he'd utter at 4 am were very often, "It hasn't come yet; can't be long now," and then the rest of the day would be punctuated with tales of every operation he'd previously undergone. The operations took precedence over the purpose behind them. He'd had an operation on his stomach, although he never said what it was for, and he'd boast about how he was put on a table and sliced straight open, his intestines then taken out and thrown in a bucket. He'd be positively beaming as he stressed the point that the surgeons had never seen such a severe case and he was always keen to mention that there had only been a slim chance of survival.

To say that George was prone to exaggeration is an understatement. Another of his tales was of the time he had "the camera" down his throat during a cancer scare. He got the all-clear, but he insisted on dramatizing the situation by remarking that it was the same camera they had used to do rectal examinations on others. Then there was the time he had to go to A&E with a slight eye injury after a fight. In this story, they took his eye out completely at the hospital, but he could still see through it while it was swinging about halfway down his chest. He was a medical fantasist, but his stories were often believed. One day, an old fella visiting the farm was left in shock after George informed him that he was having both his legs amputated and would never walk again. I put the man straight by telling him not to believe a word George said. The old boy was not alone. George spun his yarns everywhere he went and because he appeared to be a genuine character in every other way, people took him at his word. Eventually, the realisation would hit, and people would be left wondering if the George they thought they knew even existed… he'd suddenly become a scarily unknown man.

It's fair to say that George did have some genuine aches and pains, and his legs were eventually operated on, but the possibility of him having deliberately aggravated the situation just to make sure he would need an operation couldn't be ruled out. He'd overload himself carrying things and he'd often go the long way around just to make things harder for himself. He also tended to take the route that involved a jump down onto concrete from a metre high – something that would rattle anyone's bones after a while. If he'd taken it easy and looked after himself a bit better, then his pains may have been manageable without surgery, but George being George, he no doubt didn't want to run the risk of missing out on an operation.

At one point, George took to walking around backwards as he found this made the pain in his legs less severe. He'd still be rushing around, never sitting still, but because he couldn't see what was coming, he'd constantly startle himself without any effort having to be put in by the others. It was quite a disturbing sight. If he'd been an animal, he'd have been put down out of kindness. In those days, there was no manager to look after people like this, no HR department – they were just laughed at.

After his latest hospital fix, George would be content for a while, but it never lasted long. He needed constant drama in his life. If he didn't have a life-threatening disorder to go on about, he'd find something else, and this would often be his wife's or his neighbour's grave illness. George's marriage must have been a match made in heaven, either that or she'd become just like him to hold her own. He said that she'd once worn her nightgown for six months while doctors conducted every test available to find out what was wrong with her. Eventually, it was concluded that there was nothing wrong with her, at which point she'd got dressed and gone back to work. It was a good job that George could do so much overtime to compensate for the loss of income. He seemed to revel in pain and upset, so it was perhaps fortunate that his neighbour appeared to be even more unbalanced than he was. George told tales about how his neighbour had been crying on his kitchen table until the early hours of the morning. It was like a soap opera, with episodes including deaths, affairs, depression, and financial ruin to name but a few. In the end, it would all be much ado about nothing and it would soon blow over. It just seemed to be a thing they did: George would have to go work, having had no sleep at all, and his pained neighbour would then be off to get a good sleep after getting it all off his chest.

The constant stream of stories George told at work caused great amusement. He arrived in a terrible state one day and said that his cat had been raped by a stray tom, and that he'd had taken it to the vet to have its "bits" examined. He had a loose tongue, and his voluntary confessions about his sex life were often cringe-worthy and made everyone uncomfortable. For some reason, he felt compelled to tell us that in all his years of marriage, he'd never known his wife have a poo while he was in the house. This was already too much information, but he'd go on to detail the literal ins and outs of their sex life, including urinating on each other in the bath. No topic was out of bounds for George, but things changed in that department after his wife read an article about the potential dangers of certain sexual positions and their sex life appeared to dry up. From this point on, we were subjected to a running commentary on how long it had been since he'd seen his wife with no clothes on and how long he'd gone without sex. This eventually led to an ill-thought-out affair with someone too close to home for comfort.

Everyone had seen their cars parked up together after work, and it wasn't long before his marriage ended. George had to live in his car for a while, but his wife then allowed him to return to the house where, in a humorous twist of irony, she took to having a poo with the bathroom door open every morning as he ate his breakfast.

George now had a real-life drama, not a fantasised one, and it seemed to age him. Rumours about him and his sex life became rife. He was rumoured to be having sexual relations with animals, whether it was with calves looking for anything to suck on after being taken off their mothers or with the cows themselves. He did seem to mourn the death of old number 44 more than was normal, but no one wanted to spend too long thinking about why that should be. Tables were turning and George was now the one being made to feel uncomfortable.

The cows on the farm were artificially inseminated, and George was to be trained on how to do it. The process involves an arm being inserted into the cow's bottom so, needless to say, innuendos were flying and there was plenty of laddish ribbing going on. A long gown and rubber gloves had to be worn and one of the lads jokingly put his hand under the gown to poke fun at George for probably getting an erection as he inserted his arm in the cow. Let's just say his hand came back out of there in a hurry and he was no longer laughing. George tried to defend himself by saying that it wouldn't happen if people didn't play around with it… but all joking stopped.

Despite the rumours and George's unusual ways, I chose to see it as none of my business. I got along with him and, unlike Bernard, he was a hard worker and he knew he had issues. My only complaints were that he was no fun to work with when his anxieties were through the roof, and his desperate need to tell me things I didn't want to know filled my head with disturbing images I've spent the rest of my life trying to erase from memory. To this day, my mind will sometimes drift to the things he told me… and then it's my turn to be put off my breakfast.

As with Bernard, there were occasions when George caused me a load of grief, especially when he was trying to help. One such occasion was when he informed me that someone he knew had died and there was a hoard of furniture that needed to be removed and given away. My house was all but empty of furniture at the time so the more he went on about it, as was his way, the more convinced I was that I should take up the offer if he'd come along to help. I was imagining I might pick up some stylish items from a bachelor pad, but it turned out to be a 95-year-old woman that had died. Her frail and elderly son met us at the rented property which had to be emptied as soon as possible. George had meant well, wanting to help the old boy and me at the same time but, not putting too fine a point on it, the house was full of worthless prehistoric tat – and it stank of very old people. I could see the sorrow in the old man's eyes and the desperation to make things work was all over George's face, so I agreed to take a van load away to help him out. In truth, I was intending to chop it up for firewood, so when the van was finally crammed full, I was thinking about the hard work still ahead of me. To my disbelief, the old chap then produced a piece of paper on which he jotted down a list of prices before handing it to me to ask if it was fair. I passed it straight on to George and glared at him while asking what he thought. "Yeah, yeah, that's giving it away," was his answer. We appeared to have very different perceptions of the words "free" and "give away" but I handed over what amounted to a week's wages and took my van load of very expensive kindling home. I tried to convince myself that it wasn't all bad and I put some of the furniture in my living room. I had paid for it after all, but those hideous items blighted my life for years, and they were a constant reminder of George and that day.

There was another instance in which George got me good and proper. It was like being a boxer; if I let my guard down, I was in for a blow to the head. He'd been pestering me all shift about going to

The Duke that night. It was the pub's race night and he went on and on about what a fantastic evening it was and what a great time I'd have. The races took place on a big screen and only small bets were placed, so I let him talk me into going. He said it would be a laugh, and I thought to myself that if all else failed, at least there would be beer. A binge drink now and again could be a welcome escape, so I agreed to meet him there.

It was November, but it had been a warm and sunny day so I made the mistake of thinking it would be an equally mild evening. The Duke was seven miles away and the bus route only got me part of the way there, so I had to walk the rest. There was a taxi rank near the pub that I planned to use to get home as the bus would have stopped running by then and I had an early start in the morning. The pub was packed out and rowdy when I got there, and I struggled to find somewhere to stand. It was a local pub, so everyone knew everyone else – except me. To make matters worse, everyone was already drunk, so it instantly felt like I might struggle to join in with the vibe of the place. Eventually, I locked eyes with George. He was sitting with his wife and in-laws at a small table (this was before the affair) and it was clear that there was no room to spare. He looked shocked and uncomfortable to see me and it was a good while before he made his way over to me. "What the hell are you doing here?" he said, the sound of utter disbelief in his voice. The realisation that this wasn't going to be the evening out I'd anticipated hit home, but I attempted to buffer the awkwardness by saying that I'd just come for a few pints. For whatever reason, it became very apparent that George did not want me anywhere near his family. He whispered out of the side of his mouth that he'd get me a pint, and then he handed it to me in a secretive way as if we were spies making some kind of covert handover, keeping his back to the others at the table.

I drank the pint as I watched the racing. As soon as I'd finished, George reappeared with another, sliding in with it held close to his chest. I was confused, but a few pints later and I was also quite merry. I told George I was off to The Heart, another pub nearby. He looked more than a little relieved. Had I imagined the whole day of pleading requests to join him at the pub for race night? The Heart was quiet and peaceful, and I continued to drink more than is wise simply because it felt like such a welcome relief after the weird carry on at The Duke. A little later, I staggered out of the boozer and made my way to the taxi rank. It was closed. I rang the number from the telephone box, only to get an answerphone as I discovered that the business operated on advance bookings only. I was tired and I had a 4 am start looming, so I decided to walk to the farm (it was only a couple of miles away) and sleep there in the hay. When I arrived, the smell of the slurry hit me – I had not thought this through. My eyes watered with the stench as I climbed up into the hay bales, and the sweat I'd worked up on the walk soon led to shivering as the cold night air reminded me that I'd stupidly gone out wearing only a jumper. I was freezing, and I was getting a headache. Moving some bales around to make a tunnel must have disturbed one of the farm dogs and the farmer was soon out yelling, "Who's out there?" as it barked its head off in my direction. I held my breath and said nothing. What on earth was I doing?

After the longest and coldest night in my life, I sneaked out of the hay and pulled on some overalls to merge into the usual routine. I was feeling rough and more than a little downhearted. Ultimately, I had myself to blame, but if it hadn't been for George, none of this would have happened. The only small consolation I had was that George had perplexingly paid for most of my evening.

Finances were not a strong point with George. He blew his wages every week without fail. He bought things that were too expensive, including cars that were beyond his means, and he had several credit cards that were constantly maxed out. He was destined for a poor retirement. His wife had him signed up to payment plans for everything from holidays to Christmas hampers, and when they couldn't make the payments, they'd be cancelled, and all the money already paid in would be lost. Bizarrely, George was always pleased when this happened, and he'd laugh at the prospect of not having to make the payments anymore. I don't think he grasped the fact that he'd lost the money that he had already paid in and he had nothing to show for it.

George, it transpired, could not read or write, and like Bernard, he would have benefited from help rather than ridicule. However, at the time, I tried to get along with him and carry on regardless of the many upheavals he put me through. With hindsight, I began to realise that in doing so I was just setting myself up for repeated blows to the head. The time I allowed him to take from me and waste is now something I look back on with regret.

The Brazen Lads

I worked with many young men on farms, generally in their teens or early twenties, and I found most of them to be embarrassingly late developers in many ways. There's a saying, there is always most pushing where there is least room, and this was certainly fitting when applied to the average young, arrogant, big-headed farm lad. Their egos were swollen beyond belief and their confidence far outweighed their abilities. They would be oblivious to any reason for being a farm labourer in the first place, failing to recognise that it was because they had not excelled at school or shown any interest in any available apprenticeships. They were "problem" children, and it was often their parents that had found them a job on the farm; a job in which no qualifications or experience were required.

These lads were mostly exempt from the early morning starts, mainly to guard against the disappointment of them not turning up. They worked 9-5 and when they arrived, they seemed to head straight for the tractor work, no doubt thinking that all other jobs were beneath them. Tractors were exciting. Sitting in a powerful machine and thundering down the country roads at full speed was a power trip for them, but they were blissfully unaware of how they were perceived by others. They may have had a roaring engine and flashing beacons on the roof, but the trailer of manure they were carting along the road was not, as they may have believed, as important as an ambulance or fire engine.

I would always advise caution whenever confronted with a large powerful tractor on the road. If you look into the glass cab, you'll often see a 16-year-old lad with poker-dot eyes pretending that he's a monster truck driver wowing an audience. They're often wearing overalls supporting the brand of tractor they're driving, and there may even be a matching cap. It's an imaginary uniform, worn to make the job look specialised and important. What it really is, is dangerous. These are school-leavers playing in heavy-goods vehicles. They're getting behind the wheel of vehicles that can have the same weight, length, and horsepower as the trucks you see on the motorway and there are no sixteen-year-olds driving those.

Meanwhile, the older and wiser workers would stay on the farm peacefully attending to the mundane duties, mindful of the fact that these jobs require the qualities that young lads lack; patience, endurance, determination, and pride in doing a job properly. They had no reason to envy being bumped and jolted about in the tractors (which have no suspension) and they'd just be glad to get the lads out of the way.

At the end of the day, the lads would park up the tractors, but it was hard to watch. The combined brainpower did not match the horsepower, and there was zero coordination. The first one back would slew his tractor across the yard and then he'd dismount and disappear around a corner. The next would arrive and be blocked by the first, but he'd just climb out and disappear. A third and fourth would arrive, and they'd simply abandon their tractors and trailers leaving the yard gridlocked. Inevitably, a lorry would arrive with a delivery of corn or a member of staff would try to leave and find themselves blocked in. A search would begin for the lads, but this would usually be unsuccessful and the older staff (including me) would have to get on and put the tractors away. I never did discover where the hell they all managed to disappear to.

I rarely ever gave anyone a dressing down, but this clown act had to stop. I'd hear the tractors arriving and I'd rush out to catch them. The cab door would open and I'd yell, "What the f***ing hell are you getting off the tractor for? Stay on and park it up!" but they just seemed to find this funny coming from me and no offence was taken. The message never did get through, no matter how much I kept hammering it home, and they would constantly park in the way of something. If they didn't, it was purely by chance. They couldn't see past the end of their noses. I once saw a lad park a tractor in the way of a second tractor. He needed the second tractor, but it was only after he climbed out of the first and into the second that he realised he'd blocked himself in. He climbed back into the first tractor to move it, this time leaving it in front of the gate – the gate he'd need to exit through. It wasn't until he was back in the second tractor that he realised he'd blocked the gate. Back into the first tractor he climbed, this time blocking in a third tractor that was about to move... It was bad enough when they were doing this to themselves, but it was beyond annoying when someone else ended up having to sort it out for them.

When young lads work together on farms, they can not help falling out with each other constantly. This may seem a harsh thing to say but, seeing as I was the one stuck in the middle of these daily childish disputes, I should know. They would be jealous of each other and they'd get carried away by the smallest of things. They seemed to exist in a world of paranoia and look at the world through tunnel vision at best. They were obsessed with each other's business, going so far as to check everyone else's wages against their own to make sure there weren't any differences. They religiously kept tabs on each others holiday entitlement to make sure no one had more time off than they did. Their business should have been with their employer, not with everyone else. They'd strut around displaying huge self-confidence, but these petty comparisons were a sure sign that it was all a front. They clearly didn't have the confidence to manage their own business.

Keeping score on who was late to work was a particularly petty pastime, especially considering they themselves did not have to start at 4 am like the die-hard staff. They'd start at 9am and would always arrive within a couple of minutes of each other anyway, it was neither here nor there, and all it took to make any difference was hitting a red traffic light. But whoever was there first, having no doubt gone through on green, would be ready and waiting with a "late again" jibe. Petty as it was, it caused real tension that would linger all day, and it did nothing to help the mood of those they were joining who had already been at work for five long hours. There were times when the only way to stop the jibing was to split them up onto separate jobs – each one then convinced that the other had plotted against them to get the easier job, switching their jibing to ranting about that instead. Neither one would ever stop to think that maybe they had the easier job themselves.

I was once caught in the middle of a which-tractor-is-best standoff. One lad was saying John Deere was best, the other saying it was New Holland. There was no reasoning behind any of it, it was just an argument – and not unlike a playground "is, isn't" battle. They were staring into each other's eyes, incensed by what the other said and at loggerheads. It looked like it might get physical, demonstrating their immaturity and inability to respect anyone else's opinion. I had to diffuse the situation with a bit of humour, suggesting they should get themselves into bras, knickers, and lipstick if they were going to carry on with their catfight. This had the desired effect; the standoff was diffused, but they took to laughing at me instead, totally unable to see that the joke was on them.

My fight calming skills were wasted on them, and later in life, I chose not to intervene in such infantile disputes. Maybe taking the heat out of a situation for them was not helping them to learn the stupidity of their ways in the long run, and maybe punching one another in the face was just a part of the learning process.

Since they could not get on with existing colleagues, it should come as no surprise that whenever a new lad came to work on the farm, they did not get on with him either. On a new lad's first day, they would find themselves being stared at intensely. I was usually there to break the ice and start conversations, but heaven only knows what it must have been like when I wasn't there. The outrageous gaping was embarrassing. This was not a fleeting sideways glance to check out the newcomer while going about their business, this was full-on staring. They would stand, motionless, gaping with mouth ajar, faces blank of any other expression, just gawping. Much of this staring was directed at the newcomer's wellies and boiler suit. This was big boy sh*t. Brands and styles were status symbols. Basic Dunlop wellies might be in the £5 a pair price range, but Land Masters could be up to £50 a pair. If he had on an expensive pair, he'd be subjected to, "Who does he think he is?" comments, but if they were a cheap variety, he wouldn't be considered a threat. Overalls that were nondescript or had been acquired from somewhere else with an unknown company logo sewn on them were accepted, but if they were tractor branded, then this could be a territorial threat – and a which-tractor-is-best standoff could be on the cards. Truly, it was like watching animals reacting to each other, and similar behaviour could be seen when a new cow from the market was first put in with the herd. The only difference was that there was no sniffing from the lads, although there was sometimes slavering. When the weighing-up process had taken its course, work would begin.

I'd take some responsibility (when I was there) and get the new lad settled into an easy job that would keep him busy until lunchtime. Something comfortable and not too taxing on the brain, so that new surroundings could be taken in. I'd show him the clocking in machine and make a new card with his name on it, and ask if he'd brought anything for dinner or if he'd need to be taken to the bakery… all the little things that someone was going to need to know and couldn't simply guess. This should have been standard practice whenever someone new arrived but giving assistance or showing any kind of hospitality was not the way of the brazen lads. The newbie would be thrown in with the expectation that the lads would show him the ropes, but they'd be having none of it. They'd unanimously decide that the newcomer was stupid, a decision based on him not knowing where anything was. How could he know? This demonstrated just how thick and ignorant these young lads were. The newbie would be sent to refuel a tractor, but they wouldn't think to tell him that there was a lock on the diesel tank. He'd return to ask where the key was only to be met with looks of disgust and disbelief and a finger being pointed in a vague direction, "There!" Much searching would follow as the poor newbie wouldn't dare ask for clarification. The keys were often hung on nails hammered into beams so that they'd be out of sight. How the hell could anyone know these things without being shown? No-one could know where all the keys were kept for doors and gates or where all the switches were to activate lights and water pumps or where every piece of equipment was kept, but this rubbish would go on until an adult intervened.

I tried to remind the lads that they had once been the newbie, saying, "Did you know any of that when you first came here?" but this fell on deaf ears. They couldn't remember how it felt to not know. Things would eventually improve because sooner or later the lads would fall out with one another over something petty and then both camps would want the newbie as their friend. It was noticeable that none of this ever happened if the newcomer was a grown man. The bully tactics were only ever used on their more vulnerable colleagues – this said it all.

These lads had a lethal cocktail of attributes: young, bold, brash, big-headed, and thick. It made conversation between themselves into a challenge, but when a third party was involved, it was embarrassing. On occasion, the third party would be the vet. Highly educated and focused on the job, vets want to talk about business and dispense advice on what needs to be done. They charge a lot of money and they don't want to be casual about an appointment, they are there for a purpose. There were many times when the vet would be explaining the diagnosis to the farmer and the lads would notice his presence and make a beeline straight for him. As they saw it, this was an opportunity to mindlessly converse with someone different. Oblivious to the professional conversation they were interrupting, they'd intervene with an opening line such as, "Wot you doin' with a Mazda, they're sh*te!" The vet would only need to give it a moment's thought to realise what he was up against. "It's four-wheel drive and good for the kids," would be a standard and polite reply. "How can you stomach putting your arm up cows' arses?" was pretty much guaranteed to be the next question, followed by, "How much do you earn in a week?" At this point, the vet would be gone, but the lads never made the connection between their appearance and the vet's sudden departure.

On Another occasion. I witnessed a chubby faced lass ask one of the lads to take her out on a date. They got on well together and she adored him, their banter was bordering on flirtatious, however the response from him was so crushing that it crushed her and me alongside. "why would I want to go out with you when I have a thin girlfriend, you are fat and ugly". He was not trying to insult her. He was just thick and ignorant, he was incapable of being diplomatic or subtle. He could have just said no, I already have a girlfriend but instead of that, his whole thought process came out with it. The lass was good looking, it was just that she did not fit the image of a barbie doll which many of the lads seemed to think was normal.

Communication skills were lacking, and prejudice was rife. In those days, racism was more prevalent across all areas, including on TV, but perhaps particularly so in farming circles simply because "outsiders" of any sort were rarely seen. Some might say that people didn't know any better because society was different, but I can remember feeling it wasn't right, even as a child. I also remember relatively well-educated people using racist language as if it were perfectly acceptable, the very same people who shout loudest about being offended by it today. It's a good thing that people have changed, but back then, I knew any efforts to get ignorant farmworkers to see someone else's point of view would have been in vain. This was mindless racism. There was virtually no ethnic diversity in the surrounding area and none on the farm. It was all talk. No-one was directly on the receiving end of it, so there was no-one to argue back. They existed in a self-righteous bubble and if I'd tried to show them the error of their ways, I'd have been ostracised even more than I already was.

Tax bills would be blamed on "the blacks" because none of them worked, but shortages of work would also be blamed on "the blacks" because they were pinching all the jobs. It made no sense. At one point, the finger of blame was pointed at them for causing the population explosion, even though there wasn't one. Later in life, I'd try harder to put people straight on the subject, but only where a modicum of intelligence could be found. Traveller communities also received abuse from all angles, and I did my best to stick up for them. They are fundamentally people of moral and principle, although there will always be some that have lost their way, and they are greatly misunderstood. The traveller life can be beautiful, it treasures the natural and simple things that everyone else undervalues. Their persecution goes greatly unchallenged, and it is arguably worse than racism; they literally get run out of town.

A group of Orthodox Jews once visited the farm to watch the cows being milked. They were in full religious dress and the farm lads were in hysterics, laughing at the suits, the hats, the braided hair, and the beards… everything. Incredibly, they had no idea that this was not fancy dress. Not one of them had the wherewithal to recognise the Jewish faith, and I shudder to think what the visitors must have thought. It was times like this that I felt very alone.

Anyone of any religion would be misunderstood by the lads. Any mention of Jesus, the Bible, or going to church would prompt sniggers and the passing of knowing glances between them as they instantly pigeonholed the speaker into the insane category. So much for respecting people's religious beliefs. The beauty of hope, faith, and prayer would be instantly drowned out by ignorance, and after seeing their attitudes, I chose to remain a closet Christian. Of course, when a wedding was taking place, they'd all pile into the church and sing hymns like nobody's business. At these events, all the atheists seemed to find religion perfectly acceptable, and the same could be said of Christmas and Easter – although the religious significance was no doubt lost to gifts and chocolate.

It's always said that Christmas is a time for children. One year, the lads started trying to organise who would work when over the Christmas holidays. This was in October. I was asked about 200 times what my preferences were, so it was safe to assume that they'd get everything organised amongst themselves by December. With hindsight, there should have been a written rota drawn up. When the time came, it became painfully apparent that they'd organised eff-all. They all took a staggering two weeks off (coinciding with the school holidays) and it was left to the older staff and me to cover the lot. The brazen lads all pretended to be hardened men, but they all abandoned their posts when Santa came.

Religion was only one "difference" the lads mocked. They also openly laughed at disability. Anyone different from themselves in any way would be ridiculed. This included students. In the lads' minds, anyone going to college must be stupid. After all, they'd been clever enough to leave school when they could, and their farm work was deemed far more important than any further education could ever be. They appeared to think that anyone choosing to remain a student was simply trying to avoid doing any real work. I don't think they considered the fact that there were plenty of careers that involved many years of study. It was no wonder their development was so slow; they never learned from anyone or anything that was not in their bubble. Not only was I a closet Christian, but I was also a closet graduate. I was academically educated but also educated enough in life to realise the benefits of keeping that quiet.

One morning, one of the lads discovered what looked like human sh*t on a lane near the farm. No-one knew (or would admit to knowing) who did it, and it was most probably someone caught short on their walk home from the pub or some other set of circumstances like that. However it came to be there, it became the only topic of conversation for weeks to come. This was quite amusing at first, but it then became more than a little worrying. The lads would crowd around the offending log, scratching their heads and racking their brains as they discussed every possible explanation for its existence. Everyone in turn was questioned and accused, including me. It seemed that every time I looked over, there were at least three of them standing around it, surmising. They even started taking people across to look at it – the milk tanker drivers, delivery drivers... The longer it went on, the more disturbed I became. It appeared to be the biggest problem they'd ever encountered and the most puzzling, brain-straining challenge they'd ever had to get their heads around. This got me thinking. There were lads of the same age out there in colleges and universities using their brains to study law and medicine. Thankfully, the notorious turd met its demise when the farmer blew his top and destroyed it by driving the Land Rover over it. He had calculated that the time lost to them congregating and debating around it was costing him twenty pounds per day.

Horse People

Horse owners are amongst the worst offenders when it comes to pestering farmers. I came to loath the f***ing things with a passion, the horses that is, but by default, I didn't always have a lot of time for their owners either. If a horse fogie approached me about bringing a horse onto the farm today, I'd hold up a crucifix and start talking in tongues, hoping they'd run for the hills. I have been plagued half to death by horses, and they were never anything but a thorn in my side. Farming is work and horses are leisure. They might often share the same location, but they are poles apart. The problem with keeping horses for leisure is that there's a load of hard work involved, and that is not leisure. It also takes knowledge to keep the land and common sense to care for the animal, but many horse fogies just want to ride the horse and the rest of the baggage gets left behind. Keeping horses is expensive. If the keeper is not well off, then keeping a horse is not going to be elegant. You see horses dotted around the countryside taking up all the small screwy corner fields and banking fields that are too small to be of any use to the farmer. Modern machinery simply can't get into them, and they were probably hen hut fields in the olden days. These get scrounged off the farmer, but they are usually insufficient spaces. The grass soon disappears, the ground gets worn away to bare soil, and then the asking of the farmer begins... hay or haylage is going to be needed as a grass substitute. This is all well and good if it's paid for and the horse will eat it. Usually, the horse would pick and poke at it and end up wasting most of it by sitting on it, sh*tting on it, and eventually leaving it in a rotting mound. The keeper of the horse would then start questioning the quality of the bale, demanding the next one for free as compensation.

These horse keeping sagas would always begin in the good weather months. Keeping a horse must seem desirable in the summer, but winter soon comes around and then the horse needs a shelter. At this point, the farmer will be asked how to go about it, a problem shared is a problem halved as they say, but it would inevitably all come down to how much the keeper wanted to spend. This was usually nothing. An old, shabby Royal Mail lorry container will then appear, one that was probably free if removed. I have never actually seen a horse go into one of these containers, even in a blizzard, but they get filled with metre-high straw bedding and hay in preparation for use just the same. Meanwhile, the horse chooses to stay outside and just stand at the side of it, using it as a shield from the wind. As the field begins to resemble a desert, things start to get desperate, and the horse fogie will then start asking the farmer about reseeding the field so that there is more grass. This would be a nightmare for the farmer. The gateway would probably need to be widened, the field would need spraying to burn everything off, then ploughed, rotavated, seeded, rolled, and then sprayed again to clean out the weeds when growth started. The soil would probably be thin and full of stones anyway, hence the piece of land not being used for anything else in the first place. I have seen farmers do such things in an attempt to satisfy the horse keeper. Perhaps it's because the farmer, typically male, might choose to treat the horse keeper, typically female, a little more politely initially and not wade in with the usual bluntness, but more fool them. After considerable effort and damage to machinery, the reseeding process is counterproductive. The area is still not enough, and the grass will be eaten straight off leading to the same mess as before. Worse still, the horse needs another field to go into while the reseeding is done, somehow instilling the idea that this field can be freely used as well as the other.

Soon enough, horse fogies will begin to come and go as they please, asking the farmer if they could just top the water buckets up whenever they need to head off somewhere for a few days. The next ask is if the farmer could throw some hay in and keep an eye on it… who is it that wants to keep this horse? I always think the poor horses look so miserable. They mule and stand motionless in the rain, sometimes just facing the wall so that they can't see anything. They are prisoners. There's no freedom, and they effectively only get out for a one-hour ride once a week. I'd often look at these horses and wonder if they wouldn't be better off dead than alive. Eventually, the horse would disappear. Some eager and unwitting soul would have bought it after the last one had had enough of it. The field is then left, now bald with massive random patches of dock weeds (these seem to follow horses), a big pile of rotting hay, and the old box van left half-full of rain-soaked bedding. Before the horse's arrival, this was an unnoticed dormant grey field, but after its departure, it's a labour-intensive, clean-up operation – and an eyesore. It's also now known as a horse field, leaving the farmer vulnerable to more horse fogies asking after it.

There are, of course, horse owners who also own land and stables. This variety is much less troublesome to the farmer, but they can still be somewhat of a nuisance. They too would ask the neighbouring farmer about reseeding their field, but they never seemed to understand how much time and effort this would require, asking as if it might be done for them as some sort of favour. Their fields always got into a lousy state with dock weeds and nettles. "Are you running a dock weed farm?" I'd ask them, but I don't think they ever caught on to the fact I was implying their fields were a disgrace. The amateur horse keeper does not have the same common sense a farmer has, and they often have a career that has institutionalised them. This is where the money comes from, but it's also where the common-sense is drained out. I'd constantly be asked for my opinion on matters, but my advice would seldom be taken. Once, I was asked if I thought a vet was needed for a horse. I couldn't see anything wrong with it so I questioned why they thought a vet should come out. The horse owner didn't know, they just "had a feeling" something wasn't right. The vet came, gave the horse a thorough examination, and concluded there was nothing wrong with it. The owner was relieved, but it was never long before the vet was called back out again – and there was never anything wrong with the horse. The reason for the call-out might be a runny eye or a minor cut, something that didn't merit professional treatment, so the vet must have made a fortune out of it. I got the distinct impression that the whole rigmarole of keeping this horse was some sort of drama release system. These dramas always seemed to unfold on the weekends or days when the owner was off work. There were never problems after the owner had had a hard day at work, indicating where the real issues may have been. Expensive speciality feeds were used and all kinds of supplements, vitamins, minerals, oils, and hair treatments. What an almighty palaver, and all of it unnecessary. The poor horse would have been no worse off had it simply been left alone.

I refused to supply this horse keeper with any hay, straw or haylage. They had no perception of what was good stuff and what was not, so just to be on the safe side, they insisted that everything was no good. Everything was either too dusty or, for some other unspecified reason, the horse just wouldn't eat it. I pitied the guy who became the supplier. Deliveries were restricted to weekends, and then he'd need to return to fetch most of it back again when it was rejected. Had a delivery been allowed during the working week, there probably wouldn't have been any complaints made, it was all just part of these horsey folk milking the drama out of their time off on a weekend. They did ask me to supply the hay, saying they were not satisfied with what they were getting, but I looked at the hay they had and told them straight that it was the best hay I had ever seen and nobody would be able to better it. It wouldn't have mattered what they had, I just didn't fancy being the one that had to return for rejected bales with the band or netting already taken off.

Something I will never understand is why people want to keep horses. I've heard it said that it's a status thing, but I simply cannot see this. What status does it bring to have a horse? It gives me the opposite impression; more like short-sightedness and stuck for something to do. Many of these people empty their bank accounts and end up skint by keeping the stupid things. It's like paying to work instead of getting paid. Horses do nothing other than damage land, leaving a mess of weeds and stinking piles of sh*t everywhere. The keepers often know nothing about animals, making everything an unnatural struggle for them, and this has the knock-on effect of people like me being constantly pestered and annoyed by questions. It confuses me even further to think that the whole point of keeping a horse is to ride it, an activity that I've tried and found to be incredibly boring, with the majority of rides becoming little more than a procession of trying to get around people with dogs while people in cars try to get around you.

Horses are a relentless inconvenience on roads and lanes. All over the countryside, people are walking with their crackpot yapping dogs that yank at their leads. They are on every lane and around every corner, and horses do not like unfamiliar dogs. When riders on horses meet walkers with dogs, there's often too little space to pass safely. The horse is limited in the amount of manoeuvring it can do, so it's up to the dog walker to realise this and get themselves out of its way. This inevitably involves much tugging at leads and fussing to get the dog to stay by their side, adding to the building tension and nervousness that can be seen in the horse's body language. Having negotiated the dog walker, the horse rider will undoubtedly face another dog walker within a minute... These "get pasts" are not always friendly affairs. The dog walkers may not understand that they need to do the manoeuvring, space awareness seemingly a widely unfamiliar thing, meaning that the horse rider must then ask them to step to the side – and here lies the problem. No matter how politely it's done, this ask can seem unfriendly, and a dog walker's nose can be put firmly out of joint at being asked to move out of the way. As they see it, it's the horse that's in the way and their liberties as a walker are being encroached, often resulting in a deliberately unfriendly response to the ask.

The utter joy of horse riding extends beyond negotiating walkers to negotiating vehicles. Horse riders must surely know that public highways will have vehicles on them, so is there any place worse to ride a horse? Vehicles constantly get stuck behind horses, the drivers staring at the arses of both horse and rider for eternity as they wait until it's safe to pass. I do believe that some horse riders are on a misguided power trip, not unlike the brazen lads in their tractors, thinking that people are looking at them with desire and wonder. They are not. Most will be thinking something much more along the lines of, "Why don't you get off the road with that f***ing horse and stop causing a traffic jam, you silly bitch"

Horses are dangerous, just ask the accident and emergency department at any hospital if you don't believe me. They are heavy and strong animals that can kick and bite, and they can throw a rider off at speed. The result of a fall can be devasting enough, but if the same heavy, strong animal continues to stomp all over you once you're down (albeit accidentally) the damage doesn't bear thinking about. Horse fogies delude themselves into thinking they have a special relationship with their horse and that the horse is their friend, but I'd advise considering the size of a horse's brain. Horses are animals that operate on instinct; they have big bodies and long legs that are being controlled by a relatively small brain. This makes them dangerous. A horse doesn't reason before reacting, it simply reacts on instinct, and the instinctive brain of a horse sees everything (even empty crisp packets) as a threat they must flee from.

Once upon a time, the power of horses was harnessed as a means of transport. That requirement has long since been superseded by vehicles, so I can't understand why we still have them around. I think many horse riders choose to remain blinded to the dangers, glossing over the constant danger of falling off or the horse falling on them, or the on-going risk of the animal getting spooked and doing something erratic – or just going outright nuts at random. On top of this, the horse is a mobile overtaking hazard and "give way traffic system" that can cause horrific head-on car crashes with devasting outcomes for all involved.

As mentioned earlier, I've come to hate horses with a passion. Of course, this diatribe is merely the opinion of a no-nonsense farmer with serious work to do, so apologies are no doubt in order for any personal offence taken by horse owners. However, my advice to anyone thinking of getting a horse is don't; get a life instead. Don't torture an animal for your recreation, and don't think you'll be admired on a horse because you won't be, you'll be scorned by most and the horse will only make you poor. If you do happen to have too much money and feel that you absolutely must have a horse (for reasons best known to yourself) then keep it at livery stables where everything is managed for you. At livery, all your complaints can go to the manager; you can pay others to feed, water, and muck it out, thereby keeping the farmer out of it. If you throw enough money at it you won't even need to trouble yourself to go out and see it.

In the days when I worked in a utility company in the town (more on this later) I was once approached by a senior manager who thought we would have lots in common after she discovered that I lived on a farm. She thought this because she had a horse. I told her that her horse was a drain on her life: a social drain, a financial drain, and a time drain and that I thought her horse was a dangerous and useless sack of sh*t. I also told her that she could ring me day or night and I would come around and shoot it dead for her as a favour. She never spoke to me again. I always wondered if she might one day come to her senses and ring me to take up the offer.

Again, apologies to any offended parties. I hate horses.

People from The Town in the Countryside

During my time on farms, I've been hindered and driven to distraction by people that have no connection with farming or the countryside. These could be intelligent, sophisticated, and perfectly normal people, however, as soon as they took the step over the threshold into a farmyard, they became clueless and useless burdens to me. It was as though they'd entered a different world but didn't realise it, stepping out of a time machine that had transported them from the distant future. Seemingly confused by the whole concept of farming, they'd start asking questions that were so simplistic they were hard to answer. Everybody's recent ancestors were farmers, but modern times have distanced people from all the things that everyone once knew, the once common knowledge no longer common at all. Modern people don't need to know about dairying, or meat and crop production, they just buy food from the supermarket. This is perfectly understandable, people don't need to know about farming, yet they insist on coming out to farms in the countryside. I'm not sure if they always know why they do it, but they do, and it's because they do that the problems begin. For me, townspeople were just another unwanted torment that I had to put up with, leaving me endlessly trying to bridge the gap of understanding between the rural and urban worlds.

I once worked on an open farm, and it was there that I suffered the most torment. Random people would come asking questions or they'd want to acquire something, usually hay or straw for their rabbit hutch. The problem was, they never seemed to know which one they wanted. It was baffling to me that anyone could not know the difference between hay and straw or recognise either one. Grown adults would see me forking silage and visibly gag, they seemed to think it was manure even though it was green and sweet-smelling, and many reacted to cow sh*t as if it had been created by humans. The visible shock and horror on their faces spoke volumes. They would look at me working away, clearly repulsed and disgusted by what they thought must be the worst job in the world. The looks of shock would gradually switch to smirks of amusement as they stared, their thoughts of, "How can he do that?" leading into assumptions and judgements over my intelligence. The overalls and wellies doubtless added to the misconception, and they would watch me as if I was giving some sort of live demonstration in a museum. The everyday tasks in hand didn't merit their fascination, serving to highlight how distanced townsfolk had become from the country ways of their ancestors. They had come to visit an open farm, so it seemed their brains clicked into tourist mode and they fooled themselves into believing they were viewing a unique and rare attraction. The fact that this was just everyday work on a farm and everything they saw was simply common practice across the industry completely escaped them.

There was (and still is) a great irony in this scenario. The townspeople look at farming and its practices as something "out there" and unusual, yet farming is closer to natural life than town life, and farming has been the norm for thousands of years. It's town life that's new and unusual and a way of life that previously didn't exist. People that now work in modern offices, institutions, and factories get exercise by joining gyms and getting on machines designed to mimic natural movements. Food, water, and power are delivered to their doors and their waste is taken away, meaning many have no understanding of where food comes from or what's involved in keeping supermarket shelves stocked – and they certainly don't have any use for a pair of wellies.

Witnessing this made me wonder how this level of ignorance came about. Farming is all around; how is it possible that so many people know so little about it? I'd have 50-year-old men and women asking, "What animal is pork from?" or, "Why are the cows kept inside during the winter?" or, "Do the calves stay in the pens all their life?" Answering these basic questions can be tedious when they're being asked by children, but no one minds educating a child. The constant stream of questions from grown adults, on the other hand, felt like a total hindrance and "for f**k's sake" was the answer I had to try very hard not to give. It always amuses me that this phenomenon has never featured in an episode of The Archers. In their world, everyone understands everything and there's never any painful confusion.

A further implication of not understanding farming is not understanding that death is simply part and parcel of keeping livestock. Death is just as natural as birth, and it happens. Livestock is usually slaughtered before getting old or ill but from time to time there will be dead stock on the farm. A percentage of random deaths will always occur when large numbers of animals are being kept, but townsfolk would often wrongly associate the sight of a dead animal with an act of animal cruelty. Passers-by would unwittingly happen upon a dead animal and their lingering over it would bring it to the attention of even more would-be passers-by. I once saw a crowd gather around a dead sheep. It had chosen to die on a footpath and great concern was being displayed by all who came upon it. Some were muttering, "Oh, you poor thing" as they cried over it and others seemed compelled to stroke it, making the whole tearful scene appear as if a murder had been committed.

For anyone who knows sheep, death is not uncommon. Sheep, it would seem, are born with just one ambition, and that is to die.

Try as you might and with every effort put into keeping them healthy, they will still manage to achieve their goal of dying. In the case of the footpath death, once the farmer had been alerted, he attempted to explain this to the gathering crowd. There could have been any number of reasons for its demise and the body would not have gone unnoticed for long because livestock is kept under regular observation. Trust me, farmers know when an animal has died, and they race to remove the body as soon as possible to avoid these situations. It would have been on his list of things to do but, seeing as the animal was dead and no amount of fussing over it was going to change that, he may have had more pressing issues to attend to first.

The cultivation of animals is not a pleasant concept but, for as long as society continues to eat meat and drink milk, it's a matter of supply and demand. On British farms, animals are looked after to high standards, ensuring the life they have is a good life. However, I was sick to death of having to explain this to people, some of them becoming distraught as they watched the cows being milked. It does look unnatural when a cow is indoors and hooked up to a machine, but then, high-bred milk cows are unnatural to start with. Milking doesn't take long, and most cows enjoy it as it relieves the building pressure in their milk bag. A middle-aged woman once gave me a hard time over it while she watched me work. I eventually asked her if she drank milk and she replied that she did. Where on earth did she think her milk supply was coming from? It seems more than a little short-sighted to give the farmer a rollicking when you are creating part of the demand he's working hard to supply.

Farm work is hard enough without the added hindrance of clueless and misguided people. It was frustrating being asked questions when I already knew the answer I gave wouldn't be understood. Another task I often undertook was the repair of dry-stone walls. I dreaded having to do this anywhere near a public footpath. People would stop and watch, again, possibly imagining

I was giving some sort of public demonstration. I'd get comments like, "How amazing!" and, "How long does it take to learn how to do that?" It was not that long ago that the job of cobbling a few stones together to make a wall was a job that anybody could do. There's no cement, it's just crossing the joints, making it no more complicated than building with Lego bricks, so why does it garner such attention? It never ceased to amaze me that the people who gushed the most were the ones living in areas where there are dry-stone walls everywhere. Any journey in the locality would reveal miles and miles of them on both sides of the road and as far as the eye could see, turning the landscape into a patchwork of segmented squares. They would look at me and see a rare and unique skill, unable to recognise that this was just another forgotten aspect of a life everyone once lived. Perhaps it was having the motivation and guts to pick up a stone and get started that was the real fascination. Anyone living an institutionalised life seems unable to understand anything that isn't accompanied by an instruction book and working procedure guidelines.

Townsfolk on farms meant constant anguish and confusion. I'd be accosted by activists when taking animals to slaughter. They'd wait by the gates and yell, "You b***ard" and, "why don't you leave the animals alone" as I drove the Land Rover and trailer through them. They didn't understand that the animals had been bred for meat. If the demand for meat didn't exist, then the animals wouldn't exist, but I never entered into conversation with any of them as the gap of understanding was too great. The mind boggles. I can only imagine they thought farm animals were natural and the farmer should devote his life to keeping them as pets for no financial gain, or perhaps they thought these animals had been caught in the wild. If they wanted to campaign against the slaughtering of animals then they needed to take the campaign to their meat-eating friends, family members, and colleagues who were creating the demand for the product.

Muck spreading also seemed to cause outrage. I'd often become aware of someone staring at me as I worked in the field. There was a time when encountering someone with a concerned expression on their face would have prompted me to stop the tractor and ask if they were okay. On those occasions, I'd be asked what I was doing, followed up with, "Should you be doing that?" The questions would then probe into the dangerous chemicals being spread and I'd explain that it was nothing more than manure. This led to yet more questions over whether I should be doing that, as if they saw it as human excrement being spread all over the field, so further explanation had to be given to make clear its source and why it was used as fertiliser. Most of my explanations were met with unconvinced looks, implying that people thought I was lying to cover something up. One man went so far as to say he was reporting me to the Environment Agency. I never heard any more about it, so I expect they told him exactly what he'd already heard from me. Such accusations of criminal behaviour were challenging. The fields were worked to make a monoculture of grass to feed the animals. They were flat and green with dry-stone walls surrounding them and I wondered if the man who felt the need to report me thought I was spreading muck all over a conservation meadow. Perhaps he felt that cow manure should be bagged up and disposed of like dog poop instead. As I got older and wiser, I'd spot these situations a mile away and ignore such people, driving straight past without so much as a sideways glance. I was quite happy to let the fire brigade or whoever they might report me to deal with them. I confess that I began to take pleasure in avoiding such aggravating nonsense. Sometimes people would wait for my approach, and I knew their assumption was that I'd stop and talk if they stared at me from the side of the road. Instead, I'd deliberately snub them, all the while saying to myself, "And that can just sod right off," or words to that effect. It was my time, not theirs, and I was no longer willing to waste it on people that would do nothing but infuriate me with their lack of understanding. I sometimes wondered what response I'd get if the tables were turned and I visited their places of work to ask a stream of inane questions about something I didn't understand. I would guess that the responses would be something along the lines of, "What has it got to do with you?" and I don't believe for a moment that any attempt would be made to humour me or give me the time of day.

Driving a tractor along the road was another everyday farming activity that had the potential to cause outrage among non-farming types. I'd encounter many strange facial expressions on the faces of walkers I'd meet, even though I was always a careful and considerate driver. I didn't drive like a brazen lad at full throttle, choosing to keep the engine just ticking over to make the journey much more peaceful and relaxed. I always gave pedestrians lots of room, and if the road was tight, I'd stop before they even saw me, giving them time to walk without feeling they were in the way. However, when the road was wide enough, I'd just drive past as normal, using the other side of the road to pass. I noticed that pedestrians would often step off the road into the grass verge or right up onto the banking when they saw me coming – even a long way off. This annoyed me as they'd stand there waiting for me to reach them, the look on their faces as I went by suggesting they felt I'd inconvenienced them. It was only after I'd gone past, they'd realise that they'd only inconvenienced themselves by squeezing off the road for no reason. The tractor was only marginally wider than a car so there was plenty of room, and the same people never seemed to react in the same way when a car was approaching. I always raised my hand to acknowledge them, seeing as they'd gone to so much effort, but I'd invariably get twisted, confused faces looking back at me. I stopped bothering after a while and just let them get on with it. It was their mistake, not mine, although there were times when I had to interact with them because the gateway they'd chosen to stand in was the very one I wanted to go through. This should have been a situation quickly and easily rectified by them stepping out of the way, but the lack of understanding was such that they couldn't see the problem. I had to open the cab door and tell them I wanted to go into the field.

Cyclists also seem to struggle with the concept of traffic flow. They often cycle almost in the middle of the road, leaving little room for vehicles to pass. This can create huge tailbacks. Tractors, cars, and lorries are forced into crawling along behind them at 10 miles per hour, wasting fuel as they wait for an opportunity to get around the gormless cyclist. Of course, there are considerate cyclists on the roads who maintain an awareness of traffic behind them and pull over at the earliest opportunity to let the road clear, it's the inconsiderate ones with no common sense that give all cyclists a bad name.

Those with no common sense follow all the rules of the highway code and they don't break the law, but they lack the nonce to see beyond what's printed in black and white and where they're making a nuisance of themselves. The roads feed the economy. Whenever a motorway has had to be closed, the estimated financial cost to the country is always reported on the news, so there must be a cost associated with all the queues of traffic building behind cyclists all over the UK. It's the old lack of understanding yet again. He or she might have the right to cycle uninhibited and carefree on the roads, but there's a kind of ignorance that makes them unable to see they are obstructing business and people at work while they are at leisure. The country can't run on pedal power. There was a time when no-one would dream of holding up a line of traffic behind their bicycle, but those days have well and truly gone. As time goes on, it's a problem that seems to be getting worse and worse.

If common sense continues to diminish among modern-day people, it may become necessary to add everyday practical things to the National Curriculum. Things people should know may need to be taught, including how to conduct yourself when walking on the roads, which roads are suitable to ride bicycles on, and how to determine if you're obstructing the highways.

I have no problem with public rights of way, but, when you're rushing around trying to get work done, face-to-face meetings with walkers can be a nuisance. You are at work and the people approaching are at leisure. I'd always say hello, and most of the time I'd get the same in response, but there were also times when there was no response at all. Sometimes I'd get stern faces avoiding eye contact as they marched past and I found this quite irritating as I hadn't wanted to say hello either, but I'd made the effort to be polite. I will admit there were times when I muttered something along the lines of, "Well, sod you then," while they were still within earshot, but as I got older and wiser I learned to just let it go, choosing never to be the first one to speak. This was partly to save myself from the stress of getting annoyed at people, but also to protect myself from those who seized the opportunity to turn my hello into a full-on conversation. These were the walkers who wanted to gabble away to pass the time of day and enrich their rambling experience. It didn't seem to register with them that I was there doing a job and trying to earn a living while they were gabbling on and being a hindrance. It was a double-edged sword; I'd either be snubbed or smothered, but either way, it was a pain in the arse to me.

All of this will no doubt sound unnecessarily harsh, but I wasn't trying to be a grumpy b*gger, it was becoming a side-effect of having to deal with impossible people. Common sense is standard in farming, but basic things seemed not to register with many other people. I have found some of the most academically accomplished people to have the least common sense. Doctors, teachers, solicitors and so on, anyone who has been institutionalised will most likely have suffered this fate. I've been nothing short of heroic in accommodating these unknowing souls in the past and I could write a whole book about the favours I've done for such people when asked. Favours anyone else would have said no to, and favours I didn't owe or get anything back from.

One such academic was a university doctor. She saw me out mowing grass in the field and commandeered me to mow the grass in her large garden. It was so overgrown that her lawnmower couldn't touch it. I was struggling to comprehend why anyone would let the grass get so long in the first place, but as I had the mower on the tractor anyway and I could see the garden ground was flat, I thought it wouldn't be a problem. At the arranged time, I drove down the winding drive with the tractor and mower, struggling to get around tight bends and protruding bushes, only to find her car parked in the way. She had not given any thought as to how I would access her garden with machinery. I had to reverse out, a tricky task with a trailed mower. She followed me in her car, practically nose to nose with the tractor bonnet, and then I got caught in the shrubbery and almost jack-knifed the mower. I would need to go forward before having another attempt, but my signals to her in the car, which she could clearly see as she was so close, were not having the desired effect. I was waving at her to move back, but this apparently did not compute as she sat there waiting for me to move as if I was the one in her way. I had to climb out of the cab, scrabble through bushes, and explain to her that she'd need to move back to give me room. I finally made it into the garden, my trousers ripped and snagged, and my legs scratched by thorns, but the doctor had disappeared back indoors as soon as she'd parked the car. I had to knock on the door to ask her where I should put the hose pipes, plant pots, and assortment of toys that were scattered all over the garden. "Oh, I didn't think of that," came her reply. Whatever she was a doctor of, it certainly wasn't anything practical. Once the visible items had been cleared, I asked if anything else might be hidden in the grass that could be damaged by the mower – or do damage to the mower. She didn't think so, but it was hard to be convinced given her performance up to this point.

I engaged the clutch and sank the mower into the grass. A mangled Tonka toy was immediately thrown out the back. I kept going; if I'd stopped the engine the blades would have continued to rotate with momentum anyway, so I always gave a grace period after a bit of a grind. I was hoping for the best and my confidence was restored as I'd gone halfway around the garden without any further mishaps… but, more grinding sounds were yet to come as rocks and garden shovels began to get blown out of the back. I decided that adjusting the mower to a higher working level was the safest option. This was going to leave the grass longer, but I was determined not to risk the machine any further and she'd be able to finish it off with her little mower. I was dying to get out of there as the whole situation was causing me stress, but all of a sudden, an almighty crash stalled the tractor. The mower had hit a whacking great tree stump hidden by weeds in the middle of the garden. The belt had been thrown off and the tin guards were bent.

With the task finally done, I headed for the exit. "Oh, thank you so much, it looks so much better," was the doctor's response, but as I looked back at it, all I could see were bald bits, half-cut grass, patches with soil blown everywhere, and most of it not touched at all. I told her the tree stump had broken the mower but, "Oh, I am sorry," was all she had to say. There seemed to be no sense of what this meant or the inconvenience it would cause me and, "I'll get you a few pints next time I see you in the village," were her parting words as she went back inside. She seemed to deem the whole thing a success; I spent the rest of the evening repairing the mower.

It wasn't money (or lack of it) that bothered me, I just found it annoying that she'd thought of it as a favour-type job and hadn't seen my time or machinery as something that would need to be paid for. Perhaps it wasn't intentional, it was just the old lack of understanding phenomenon raising its ugly head yet again, but if I'd done something like accounting or secretarial work for her, would she instantly have considered it something worthy of payment? I think she thought driving a tractor was just part of the countryside, something that's freely there like trees and birds, and not a business proposition. It made me wonder what would happen if she did something in her job (if that's what it was) without receiving payment. It would be trade unions and tribunals all the way. I only had myself to blame back then for agreeing to do these jobs in the first place. These days, I have a list of reasons for being unavailable ready to roll off my tongue. If anyone should ask me to do some mowing, I'd reply that my mower was broken. An older farmworker once gave me some sound advice on the matter of people asking for favours. He said, "You're better saying no to them and having them think you're a miserable b*gger from the outset. They won't ask again." He was right. No matter how many favours I did for people, none of them ever invited me to their barbeques or parties. When they didn't need something done, they didn't want to know me.

Farmland boundaries are yet another area where tensions between town and country can build. In towns, there are no misunderstandings over who owns what. But when a town property borders onto farmland, the fundamentals of common courtesy seem to be forgotten. Huge piles of garden waste, frequently including dog mess, will be thrown over walls into the adjoining field. Paths will be made across the farmer's land by dog walkers, and gates will often be left open. I've seen boundary walls taken down and the stone used to make garden rockeries, and when cows have escaped, the police have been called out. I've even seen building plans submitted by people which include the use of a farmer's land. When the farmer objected, his name became dirt. The infuriating thing was that the person submitting the plans had high security around his property to protect his patch from trespassers, but he seemed to have no respect for the farmer's rights. Somehow, the farmer was branded as evil for protecting his property and not giving away free land.

I don't doubt there will have been disputes in which the farmer was wrong, but I've never personally known any. I've known residents complain when the field adjoining their gardens were harvested by the combine. It does create a bit of dust, but it's not an all-year-round activity, and it highlights the incredible short-sightedness of people yet again. If you choose to live next to a farmer's field, you're going to see tractors and farm machinery from time to time. What's more, the field was most probably the property's biggest selling point and a premium may have been paid for the open view. If farming activities such as combining didn't take place in the field, building of some sort probably would, and then they'd have something to complain about. If the farmer didn't work the field, it would become a wasteland of weeds, probably used by motorbikes or, even worse, horses – I wonder how they'd feel about an abandoned Royal Mail container blotting the landscape? Had these town residents been able to understand the countryside for just one moment, they'd surely have concluded that a day or two of dusty combining is by far the better option – yet short-sighted confusions of this sort continue.

Farm animals escaping from fields was always a great source of stress, with random people getting involved and often managing to make the situation a far more painful ordeal than necessary. The escapees put me at the mercy of whoever's property they'd managed to get into. Even when the animals strayed into a neighbouring farmer's field, the farmer in question could be difficult about it. Of course, when it was their animals that had strayed, they seemed to adopt an entirely different attitude, insisting that it was just one of those things. The worst attitudes, however, were those of the town residents. If sheep had strayed into a garden, there'd be furious people waiting to greet me. Some would go on power trips and milk the situation for all it was worth, and they'd shout aggressively at the farmworkers who were trying their best to rectify the situation. I could read some of these characters like a book. It was clear that this sort of thing and other small issues could completely overload their dull lives, and there would be much yelling and gesturing with bright red faces. I couldn't avoid being on the receiving end of it, but I could pick up on clues and tell-tale signs and signals that helped me quickly weigh up these characters and how best to deal with them.

If they were retired, then it could go two ways. One would be to take it all in their stride, the other would be to scream blue murder. Happy old couples tended to take it completely in their stride. Their home and garden would be well kept but humble, and this indicated that they were content in life and not prone to making a fuss. Such modest folks were understanding, and the sight of a cow standing in their back garden might even bring a smile to their faces. They'd often give a friendly wave from the kitchen window and not even bother to come out, leaving the round-up crew to get on with it. They had the sense to realise what had happened and could sympathise with us under the circumstances. They knew a hoof mark or two on the lawn would disappear naturally within a week or so, and that a few bite marks on the leaves would barely be noticeable before they grew back again, and even if a flower bed had been scuffed across, they found it was no big deal to straighten things out again.

On the other hand, the less content retirees, commonly those living alone, tended to have less humble homes and gardens, and the ones that looked distinctly overkept could be trouble. Some residences had gardens that had the look of a hyperactive perfectionist making a full-time job out of it. Typical indicators of trouble included novelty garden gnomes and twee signs; water features crammed in where they didn't fit, and paths leading all over the place where one would have done the job. Over painting was another little clue, where the shed and fence looked like they'd been painted weekly. In situations like this, I knew I'd be dealing with a fusspot and their over the top garden would be matched by an over the top response to the unfolding event. Incidents involving such gardens could be expensive to rectify, and the farmer would rightly pay for it, but in the heat of the moment, the outrage and wrath I had to endure was unnecessary. Livestock had escaped, but it was an accident. Sadly, some over the top reactions could be justified when it transpired that certain plants and ornaments that had been damaged were memorials to lost loved ones. These situations became unbearably awkward ordeals to sort out and I wouldn't wish them on my worst enemy.

Then there were the overgrown and unkempt gardens in which no real damage could be done, yet the owners of these properties were likely to be the biggest power trippers. Trespassing had taken place and they were about to use it to assert their authority. These characters seldom had authority over any aspect of their lives, made evident by the state of the garden, but they saw the appearance of livestock as a golden opportunity to experience being somebody important. They'd be out in a flash, shouting and carrying on, and quite often blocking the animals in but they'd be unable to see this as they were too busy creating a scene. "What the f***ing hell do you think you're playing at?" would be yelled at everyone and anyone, as if the farm staff trying to round up the animals had deliberately herded them into the garden. "You do realise you'll be paying big time for this, don't you?" would come next, but a quick look around the area was all that was needed to see that there was nothing to be paid for. The threats were empty, but they'd had their moment of shouting loudest.

If the garden belonged to a family home and toys were scattered all around it, the owners would generally be busy people with plenty of other things to worry about. Two cars on the driveway was always a good sign as people who need to get to work are much less likely to take the time to milk the situation. They have enough drama in their daily life without creating any more by blowing things out of proportion. Livestock running through the garden was not something to celebrate, but they'd generally leave the farm lads to get on with it and just be thankful that someone else was there to deal with it so that they didn't need to be involved.

The gardens said a lot about the people who lived there, but some people found great excitement in the drama of escaped livestock appearing on their property and they wanted to help. This could be every bit as annoying as being unfairly yelled at. No matter how good their intentions, people "helping" would be a hindrance. They'd rush out wearing shiny and coordinating hats and wellies, looking determined to help save the day, but they were grossly underestimating the skills needed to direct livestock. Animals can be read by their facial expression and body language, making it possible to anticipate their mood and the way they're likely to behave, but you need to understand animals to be able to read them. If animals are worked up, they're more likely to make erratic moves such as jumping a fence or barging through people. If they're kept calm, they're going to mosey along and be guided to safety. Silence is needed when livestock is being edged in the right direction, no noise means no distractions or reasons to divert, but people with no livestock experience won't know this. What is obvious to the experienced is not at all obvious to "helpers" and they invariably get in the way by shouting and trying to herd them from the front. This doesn't work. It is dangerous when inexperienced people are unable to detect the warning signals when an animal is getting into a state. They'll run up behind it, chasing it, and this can have devasting consequences. I once saw a bull being chased in this way and the situation rapidly got out of control as it headbutted and smashed a van door in its rage. A police marksman had to shoot it dead. Chasing a powerful animal is never going to end well. You can't outrun it, and you can't catch it; it's not like trying to retrieve a runaway toddler that has gone too far ahead on the pavement.

I've made the mistake of allowing willing volunteers to help me in the past, but it has rarely been worthwhile. I've had them standing in gateways to stop animals getting through, but when the animals appear, they're nowhere to be seen and the animals galivant straight through. I've had individuals help me with the simplest of tasks such as opening a gate when I gave the signal, usually to let a sheep through that need separating from the flock. When the time was right, I'd say, "Open the gate," but the opportunity would invariably be missed in the time it took for the person to think about what I'd said and then do what I'd said. What was there to think about? Sheep are not known for their deep thinking, but if they see an open gate when the time is right, they'll go through it. If they see a closed gate, they're not going to stand and wait patiently for it to be opened for them, they're gone.

There's a notoriously vicious old farmer I know who goes by the nickname of 'F***ing B**t*rd Bob' and I raise my hat to him. His bitterness is more advanced than my own and there's still much I can learn from him as he's further down the same path I'm on. When people with no livestock experience would try to help him, he'd say, "You f**k off back in the house, we don't need your help," with a heavy emphasis on the "your." This sounds unbelievably ignorant, but it has proved to be useful on several levels. Firstly, his straight-talking delivers the message instantly and bluntly, thereby saving time as there's no bumbling small talk after the statement is made. Secondly, it's insulting enough to ensure that the offer of help will never be made again, providing a safeguard for the future, and thirdly, it yields the best outcome all around as the livestock will get to where they need to be much faster and easier without the added hindrance.

Townies and Animals

When you are brought up on a farm, you can generally read animals in a way that cannot be learned from a textbook. This comes from the day to day handling of animals, worming them, treating their wounds, or trimming nails and hooves. The look in an animal's eyes and the position of its feet are subconsciously noted and monitored, so I'd always know the right moment to inject or apply the stinging ointment without even thinking about it, and I'd also know when to walk away – or sometimes even run. I only realised this was a seasoned skill after noticing that others didn't have it. The others would often be in the form of newly qualified townie vets. I'd often see a young new vet assume that an animal would just stand still while being examined or treated, so preoccupied with their diagnosis that they'd overlook the obvious. I once saw a new vet stick her hand straight under a cow without registering its bulging, staring eyes looking back at her: it kicked with precision and broke her wrist. The years of study were over, but practical reality had not yet been fully realised. Animals that are seemingly dying can find a surge of energy when they're required to stand still; I've known them to smash walls down and disappear over the horizon.

When new vets first begin visiting real-life farms on their own, the excitement can be seen in their faces. They have progressed from treating the small animals in the surgery, and they're no longer being shadowed by their seniors. They've arrived at their chosen vocational destination, and they must feel a sense of accomplishment, but there was always something about these townie vets that, as a farmer, I couldn't quite figure out. I did not doubt that these young vets were more intelligent than myself, they would have been grade A students at college and would have been aiming for the top jobs, and I'm sure their cleverness and ability would have been praised and encouraged, but I often wondered if some of them only aimed to be a vet because it was such a high ambition and they wanted to prove that they could do it. The reason I thought this was because all those years of study had only brought them to the same sh*thole places I was at. They wore the same wellies and overalls as me; they were in the cold and wet; the animals they dealt with were diseased and dying; infected wounds could smell horrendous, and the animals always defecated on demand then splattered it around with their tails. To add to this, the farmers would always be hard to deal with. What a horrible job. Did they really understand what they were letting themselves in for whilst training and studying? I don't think they could have; how could they when most of them had never before experienced the true grit of farms and farmers.

It made me wonder if the townie vet's idea of animals came mainly from their childhood pets. Their soft side showed through with affectionate looks or comments directed towards the beasts on the farm. It was not fitting, and to my eye, it indicated some kind of misunderstanding. They often had their own animal ethics which did not always relate to the keeping of animals for business. Many were blinkered to the fact that the veterinary bill might outweigh the profit of the animal. This would be in stark contrast to the farmer whose only concern was money. Farmers would often know as much as the vet but would remain tight lipped. Sometimes a vet was legally required for TB testing or sheep dipping, and sometimes the farmer would know when an animal was going to die, but they'd require the vet's diagnosis for the insurance. A new vet might take the time to go into great detail, telling the farmer how to treat an animal over the coming weeks. The farmer would already have reckoned up that it was a financial loss, meaning the animal would already be on death row. The new vets would soon learn the ropes, and I'm sure the seasoned vets would provide enlightenment on the farmers' hidden agendas and their financial costings.

Wild animals are an entirely separate entity from farm animals and pets, they are a natural wonder. There is a barrier between them and us, they do not want to interact with us, but I often noticed that townies did not think the same. I'd often find myself in the same space as a wild fox, badger, crow, or magpie. I'd lock eyes with them; they'd always seen me first and would stare straight through me, then vanish. They saw me as a predator as if I was as wild as them.

When a wild animal is injured and dying, it is part of nature. Death is just as natural as birth. I don't believe wild animals have emotions, and if they could speak, they'd probably say that it's better to die young than to fade away. However, I've frequently seen townies try to help injured wild animals, and this often begins at the roadside. Their rescue efforts are invariably unsuccessful, and sometimes unwittingly cruel. If a broken leg or wing is treated successfully, then the animal will never be the same again. Half the time they need to be kept in captivity until they die because they've been tamed in the recovery process and become accustomed to being fed, thereby losing the ability to fend for themselves. This life in captivity is a pointless burden. The animal will be a mere shadow of its former self, unhappy, and forced into being something that it did not want to be. Intervention with injured wild creatures can just prolong their death, creating more pain and distress. I'd get frustrated seeing such things, but I knew that my advice would not be understood, even if I offered it. A quick twist of the neck can be the most humane thing to do, but that would not translate into sense for those who were not in the know.

This brings me onto townies and hunting. I am not for a moment endorsing hunting. Hunting with horses and hounds should not be directly associated with farming, they have very little to do with each other and I've found most of those that hunt to be townies. Foxhunting, in particular, is commonly justified with statements such as, "It's to protect the farmers' poultry and new-born lambs." I've never understood this. Why would townies want to dress up in all the attire and kill foxes in order to protect some unknown individual's private business assets? I've often thought that it would be a bit like me volunteering to be an unpaid night watchman at some random privately-owned office block or something of the likes. Farmers are quite capable of managing their livestock, they do not rely on hunts to protect them. I do not doubt that for some, it's all just an excuse to kill for the mere sport of it. This can't be morally right. There's a social aspect to hunting that I think is the main attraction, and for most of them, the hunting is just a mindless ritual. There are others who hunt just to create a purpose for keeping their horse. To me, this seems a bit like buying some crutches, then breaking your legs so that you can use them. If you think outside the box, it really makes little sense, but I don't find hunting types to be thinking outside the box types of people.

The majority of townies don't like hunting and think that it's mainly the country folks that do it. I've found it to be almost the complete opposite: I have never known a farmer go on these hunts. The whole thing is a big mixed-up painful jumble of misunderstanding. It has drawn me into endless conversations with muddled-up people, some of them thinking that it's the farmers that are the hunters and directing their approval or disapproval accordingly. Some hunters think that the farmer owes them something and that they have a rite of passage through their land. Others genuinely think they are acting as essential pest control, although they commonly don't catch anything at all in a whole day's hunting. The farmer knows that hunt crowd are mainly mindless onlookers, and after the hunt has gone, the walls and fences will all need to be repaired where horses and their haphazard riders have barrelled through rather than jumping cleanly over them. Nobody will want to do that for sport – it's left to the solitary farmer to clear up the mess.

Then there are the townies that buy smallholdings with the romantic idea of retiring into a little farm place. They have usually gotten rich quick in the city and then want a quieter life. It's a lovely idea, and some do make it work as they intended, others don't. There's no prize for guessing which types I had to endure. I became acquainted with a couple who bought a smallholding that would have been ideal for keeping poultry to provide eggs and chicken meat, a few pigs for pork, a goat for milk, and one or two cows for the breeding of beef. There could also have been a large vegetable patch; the place was just the right size for self-sufficiency and a slow and relaxed existence. Instead, it all got off on the wrong foot straight away when they came across some weak leverets – the hare had probably been hunted by idiots leaving the poor offspring to die. So, the couple rescued them and took them indoors, feeding them with pipettes until they were fully grown and half tame house pets. What use was there in that? The animals were nothing but burdens and stank the house out. The time and effort should have gone into growing the veg patch or something constructive, but the heart ruled the head and more and more animals in need began filling up the outbuildings. There were three-legged dogs, blind cats, and things that could not stand up. The couple created a name for themselves as soft touches, and they were then used as a dumping ground for disabled animals by the whole district. One day, the woman came across the neighbouring farmer struggling to calve a cow, she helped pull on the ropes and got it out just in time. The calf was too big for the cow's pelvis and the cow couldn't get back up after the traumatic birth. After two weeks, the cow had to be shot; the farmer did this without telling his new neighbour, otherwise, she would have wanted to keep it. She did, however, buy the calf off him to save it from going to the market. She bottle-fed it until it was a half-ton useless pet. Before they knew it, the couple had full-time jobs feeding around these animals, mucking them out, and buying food in for them to eat. On approaching their place, you could hear it before you saw it... howling and barking dogs, cockerels crowing and tamed sheep constantly bleating to be spoon-fed more corn.

They used to get me to take their manure trailer away with my tractor, empty it at my place, then take it back off for them to fill up again. They thought that I could use the waste to spread on the farm fields, but it was mostly new straw and hay which takes a long time to rot down, and it was full of dog sh*te and random rubbish that I kept telling them not to put in. I tipped it into a pile to rot, then I had to load it back up and spread it on the fields six months later. They pestered me to roll their land which was poached up by the big dumb pet cow, and they pestered me to help bodge up their fencing and walls. It was depressing helping them because I knew there was no constructive outcome to it other than appeasing their misjudgement. We were friends for a while, but it wasn't sustainable They didn't appreciate the magnitude of my favours and even started taking me for granted. Humouring them was hard work; they actually thought that they were running a small farm.

When people are not brought up with farming, then try to do it, they never quite seem to be able to fully adapt into what it takes and what it needs. Sometimes they misunderstand what it actually is. The hard-line business survival is missing, and personalities are often too soft, polite, and domesticated. When I was young, these types plagued me to death. They needed to lean on me for the common-sense knowledge they didn't have, and which they could never seem to learn. If I could only turn back time, the favour requests and pleads for my help would be met with a stern NO! It was all a waste of time, and nothing came out of it other than unnecessary work for nothing. They were causing themselves pain and roping others into it. If I was faced with such requests today, then I would give a response in the same spirit as F***ing B**t*rd Bob.

The Milk Round and the Bean Tin Explosion

This episode is a typical example of how I was so severely tormented by idiots and it shows the strength of my youthful kindness and generosity which left me so vulnerable to them. It was a week of intense exposure to strange townies, confused farmworkers, and bad timing. It was a fast-track piece of learning for me and I was never the same again afterwards. I think you will agree that it couldn't be made up.

It all started very early one morning when I was milking cows. A milkman that I vaguely knew came to see me and he asked if I would do his milk round for him while he and his wife went on holiday. He told me that he couldn't find anybody else to do it, and he also said that if I couldn't help, he'd skip the holiday and just retire the following summer so that they could get away without the constraints of the milk round. I was self-employed at the time and I couldn't see a reason not to do it, so I thought why not? It would fit in nicely before the busy silage time when I'd be in high demand on several farms, and I wanted to help him, so it was agreed that I'd do it for the last week of May.

I never really fancied working a milk round of my own. I'd been offered several before and always turned them down. It was quite fascinating to imagine how tying it must be to deliver milk six days a week and how incredibly dull and repetitive it must be. I wondered if milkmen and women ever got sick of hearing the bottles clinking together. The early mornings in the abandoned streets always seemed depressing to me, and the pettiness of going to someone's house with a bottle of milk for a few pennies profit was unappealing. This was partly why I'd accepted the job; I wanted to see what I'd missed out on and I was hopeful that it would be all I expected of it. I thought that I'd feel smug, knowing that I was only doing it for one week. I knew milkmen that had been doing the same round for twenty years and more, so I thought the experience would be food for thought.

I had assumed that I'd be given a clear map with the orders written on it – and I'd assumed it would be easy. However, a month before Harry's planned holiday, he called to ask me to join him on his round for a practice run. I said I didn't think it would be necessary, but he insisted, saying he'd pay me, so I went along. I didn't know Harry well, and I'd also stupidly assumed that he was a "normal" person, but when I got into his milk truck I began to wonder. It was unreasonably immaculate. Harry began by saying, "Before we start, I want to show you this little plastic bag on the gear stick." I looked down at it, thinking to myself that he was over-complicating things. He continued, "I want you to put all the bits of wastepaper and messages in there so it's all neat and tidy." I looked at Harry. He was a hyperactive little man with octagonal blue-tinted glasses, and it came to my mind that he was someone who was always making mountains out of molehills and forever busy fussing over nothing. It dawned on me there and then: I had overlooked his nutcase character. When was I ever going to learn? I should have known better. Harry was a townie milkman and we were bound to have different ways of thinking, but his "ways" made the milk round utterly confusing. He had made arrangements with his customers to leave him signals that let him know whether they wanted one bottle or two. One address had an old set of weighing scales in the window; these were left balanced for two bottles and weighted to the side for one. Another had a bizarre metal sculpture in the porch. It was positioned according to the requirements, but it looked symmetrical to me and I could never see any difference. This was 'Harry's World'. I asked him to write it all down for me, and I thought I'd better go with him on the round a few more times. The following week, Harry brought pages and pages of scribbled notes that he'd obviously put some serious time and effort into preparing for me. It may have made sense to him, but it was just pages of incomprehensible nonsense to me, entirely tailored to his eccentricity. He had gone into immense detail explaining the minor things but then missed major details such as addresses. He assumed knowledge in certain places and not in others, but how he came to these assumptions was a mystery to me. I suggested just giving his customers a set delivery for the week that I'd be doing it. Harry's jaw dropped and he inhaled for ten seconds. It was a definite no! Mrs Jones has one banana yoghurt every other Wednesday, and Mr Fanny has alternating semi-skimmed and full-fat milk each consecutive day. Mr and Mrs Bottomley will greet you every morning and choose, then pay. Miss Applejack has a bag of potatoes on a Tuesday and six eggs on a Saturday… it went on and on. Harry's fusspot ways had made what should have been a simple job into a nightmare. He had set no boundaries, and anyone normal would have drawn the line somewhere. The constant curveball orders were only making him pennies, nothing more, and it seemed to me that some of his customers were setting him challenges. They had a different order for every day of the week, and then there were days when they mysteriously ordered nothing, the purpose of this perhaps being some sort of test. There were corner shops dotted all over the area, so why an earth would people bother ordering random things from the milkman? Single bananas, an odd onion, orange juice, and a flavoured milkshake to name a few. I knew why: they were using the milkman as entertainment to fill their boring lives. The milk delivery was the only event of the day for half of them, and his customers were almost all old and fussy. They were also very lonely. I always thought that townies had less family loyalty than countryfolk, with country families tending to look after their old parents, staying close to them, but most town families not doing the same. Where were their children? Had they left to live their own life, only returning for Christmas dinner? How could they just leave their old parents like this? There were streets and streets of them, all old and waiting to die. Their country counterparts were still happily working and enjoying life.

What had I let myself in for? I soon realised that every time I joined Harry on his round, he was going different ways about it. He'd drive past some customers and then make their delivery on the way back, so I asked him why this was? He said it was because he knew what time all his customers got out of bed depending on their weekly routine and he didn't want to risk the earlier risers waiting for their milk. The route alternated every day depending on all manner of things, it was preposterous, and only a nutcase adrift would have created this set-up.

On my fifth practice run, Harry decided to inform me that Mary would be helping me on the milk round when he was on holiday. I couldn't imagine that this was good news, saying, "If you don't mind me asking, who is Mary?"

"Oh, she comes with me regularly and knows the round like the back of her hand."

I could not believe this late revelation. I was confused, and had to ask, "So why isn't she doing it herself?" I was informed that it was because she couldn't drive, and this made sense, but it left me questioning why Harry had insisted I go with him to learn the round, five times now, when Mary already knew it and she would be coming with me. I was being messed about by a complete nutcase; it was the story of my younger days.

While this perplexing affair was going on, I had a new fruit loop of a friend coming to my house. His name was Tom and he had just broken up with his girlfriend, an event that had caused him to walk out of his job milking cows. He'd come and drink tea and smoke in my house, and I didn't mind too much because he wasn't asking anything of me, and he was quiet. This was quite refreshing compared to past experiences. He'd come around after I'd returned from the milk round, we'd chat, and if I wanted to sleep, it wasn't an issue. I hardly knew that he was there, he'd just come and go. He was going through a bad time and was lost. The weeks went on and my week of milk round mayhem arrived as Harry went off on holiday. I met Mary for the first time, and I could instantly see that she was not a happy bunny. She was in her sixties, she chain-smoked, her cheeks were bloodshot all over, she had insane-looking staring eyes, and she coughed a lot. She looked miserable and solemn, and she also had tinted glasses, purple this time. I thought there must be a theme going on here and, unfortunately, I started associating tinted spectacles with unstable people. Mary had no patience at all and snapped at every tiny thing. I mistakenly placed a bottle of green-top milk on a doorstep when it should have been a silver-top, and even though she watched me do it, she waited until I returned to the truck before bellowing at me, "What planet are you on?" This was not justified, and it was another little tell-tale sign that something about her was not quite right; she was a symbol of Harry's judgment. I had to pick her up every morning. She was never ready, but always said she hadn't been to bed, she smoked all the time, and was incredibly slow. I was doing most of the work, picking her up, dropping her off, and having to suffer her nasty attitude into the bargain. It was like having a diseased urchin clinging around my neck, and I really wanted to rip it off and throw it far away from me.

I returned home one morning to find Tom waiting. The phone was ringing as we went inside, and I answered it to hear Mrs Brown complaining that her milk was left in the sun on her doorstep rather than the shade. I advised her that it was dark when we dropped it off and asked her how she got my number. To my annoyance, I found out that Harry had been to the printers and had a letter made up explaining his absence to all his customers. This letter had my name and telephone number on it. What a sneaky trick to pull on someone trying to help. There was more bad news. It was the last week of May and it wasn't expected to be silage time, but the grass was ready early, and mowing began. I was now missing some of my regular work because of this painful milk round. I couldn't work day and night. I had committed myself to the round and I had to turn other work away, work that would have been easier and better paid. I took my frustrations out on Tom, asking him when he was going to move on and find another job instead of coming to my house every day. Tom was depressed and when he was at my house, he constantly poked at my fire whilst staring into the flames.

The phone kept ringing. I was getting the pettiest of complaints along with requests for tiny extra orders that wouldn't normally warrant a phone call. Complaints included things like egg yolks being pale, potatoes tasting of nothing, and one complainant said his milk tasted too milky while another wanted me to go back to his address with a pot of cream because someone had just given him some strawberries. I felt like I was being tested. I was losing money for this and risking my reputation. I couldn't satisfy these leaches, and I'd never failed to help anyone with their hay and silage when asked before now.

The next day, we embarked on the milk round at the earlier time of two in the morning, hoping to drop the milk off before the pestering customers got up, but this was largely unsuccessful. The worst offenders were already poking about, waiting for us, and some would expect a lengthy conversation, almost as if they had paid for it and expected it. Others would watch me delivering down their street and never take their eyes off me until I was out of view.

Mrs Pockleswaite would wave from her bedroom window every morning, even though she only had two bottles of milk during the whole week. I began to creep around the streets desperately trying to go unnoticed, seeing them like corridors in a lunatic asylum with people jeering and waving at me as I went past. Mary was such a nasty and slow burden that I told her to stay in the truck and read out the orders for each house, and I'd do all the leg work as it would be quicker that way. When I got home, I could hear the phone ringing before I even opened the door. It was Mr Warburton complaining that we'd left him full fat when it should have been skimmed, and then there were several more calls of a similar nature. Tom came in and started messing with the fire as usual, and more calls came. They all had the wrong kind of milk. What had Mary been doing? It had been her job to read the notes and tell me what milk to drop off all morning. Eventually, enough complaints had come in to warrant me going back out to swap all the mixed-up orders about. I thought I'd better show willing, but I was very tired and annoyed; Mary was probably asleep while I was having to go back out to clear up her mess. I shouted at Tom, "I'm going back out for the day. Nice to see you. Goodbye." He just got up quickly and left without saying a word. I'd found out that Tom hadn't told his parents he'd quit his job, and he was spending his days skulking about from place to place pretending to be at work. If I hadn't been so busy, I'd have tried to help straighten him out with some advice and helped him to find another job.

I flapped about trying to sort out the customers, wasting fuel in the process. Some were deeply annoyed and thought there was a serious case of negligence to answer, and others were looking forward to snagging me again, engaging me in conversation and holding me up just for entertainment. What an ordeal. I returned home worn out and down, only to be met with a wall of black smoke as I opened my door. The room from the roof down to the floor was filled with smoke, but in a panic, I went straight in to open a window, attempting to clear it out. I assumed there'd been an electrical fault or something like that and I nearly choked while I looked around for the fire. The carpet was smouldering but, luckily, all the oxygen had been used up, the windows had all been closed, and this had prevented it from bursting into flames. Once the smoke had cleared, I was bewildered when I saw what appeared to be baked beans all over the walls and ceiling. The fireguard also had a perfectly round hole in the mesh and there was a round indentation in the plaster on the back wall of the very same size and shape. I pieced the clues together and concluded that Tom had put a can of beans in the fire before we left the house. The explosion must have been immense as it had emptied the contents of the fireplace, scattering them all over the living room. To this day, I still can't imagine how fast that tin of beans must have been travelling to be propelled through fireguard mesh, leaving a clearly defined circle in its wake.

My sofa and chair were burnt, the carpet was ruined, but worst of all, the entire house, both upstairs and downstairs, had deposits of black soot all over it. My bed and clothes were spoilt, and everywhere smelt of burning plastic. The phone was still worked though, and it was ringing away. I rang Tom and asked him why he'd lit the fire and put a can of beans in it, telling him that the interior of my house was ruined. He never came back. The explosion hadn't been intended, he'd just been playing and experimenting with the fire, like a small child poking in the sand, and doubtless, he didn't really know what he was trying to do. I didn't bother asking for any recompense from him, I knew he had nothing, and he wasn't man enough to sort any of it out, so I'd have to do it myself. I wasn't insured, but things could have been much worse. I could have caused a backdraft when I entered the house, and it could have blown the roof off and killed me. That fate must have been only seconds away before I opened the back window.

That fateful week cost me a fortune in lost earnings, carpets, clothes, furniture, and paint. My house was almost blown up and I had to redecorate it. It had also been mentally wearing, and I'd been tormented half to death by the elderly townies on the milk round. I can only imagine that Mary's sole purpose in all this must have been to make it worse for me. It did however mark a milestone in my development. My trust and faith in people were diminishing. I was no longer quite so forgiving and non-judgmental of people, and from that point on, my home was no longer a half-way house for screwballs. I had a heightened awareness of anyone unfamiliar to me; I was turning into a sour old farmer-type. However, I was right about one thing: the milk round was a horrible tedious job, and I never looked at a milkman or milkwoman in quite the same way ever again.

Farm Kids

After first starting school, a farm child would typically start to understand that their lot was not the run of the mill. They would mix with the town kids and their parents would be modern and work in the rat race. The townies could seem socially sharp and very vocal. Some would have developed an unpleasantness harboured from an unhappy home life. Here the farm child would hear and learn things from the other kids. Things such as visits to the cinema and the sports centre or about foreign family holidays, these are things which a farm child may not yet have experienced. I personally had never left the country until I was well into my adult years, some of the kids would have thought less of me for it at the time. I was dropped off at school every day in a van, this gave some kids reason to think I that I was from a poor family, they did not understand it was for business. My clothes were slightly more old fashioned and traditional. The up to date kids had brand names across their clothing, this was all new to me. The farm kids and the town kids were different, the subtle signs were already there. School is compulsory and the typical farm kid could sometimes feel that their attendance was a legal inconvenience. In years gone by, farmers could take their children out of school at an earlier age if they were needed to work on the farm.

There are always dangers on farms, and they were much more prevalent in years gone by. Hazards could become a little over-familiar when they were brushed past every day. Corners were often cut to make things easier, things were left out so that they were on hand when they were needed. When I was a kid, there would be medicines and poisons on display, knives for cutting baler band, there would be wood choppers, spikes and forks for the hay and silage. There were belt driven turnip choppers and grain rollers, the dangers of death were real. There were ladders everywhere and asbestos roof sheets. Tractors can be death traps and animals are never to be trusted. Old walls were leaning, and all manner of things looked like they were about to collapse at any second. We were blessed in that there were never any serious accidents on the farm that I grew up on, really this was not entirely down to chance. Farm kids are told very bluntly, 'keep away from that, it will tear your arms off' and 'never go on that roof or you will fall through and end up dead' Watching the adults display caution was a good reason the follow suit and the farm kids would never need telling twice. Common sense goes a long way, young children would never be left alone, the adults knew at what stage we could be trusted. We were never going to walk behind a reversing tractor or start drinking out of the medicine bottles and we knew the things never to be done without an adult.

There were a few occasions where town kids came home for tea, I was never comfortable with this. It would be a return gesture after I had been badgered into going someone's house after school. I would go out of politeness but could never see the point int it, it was much easier and less awkward to have my tea at home and we did have our own television to watch. I was astonished to see how the town kids were micro-managed by their parents, they had to ask permission for everything. Permission was needed to get a biscuit out of the jar or to get a drink. It shocked me more than ever when I saw how the town kids had to ask permission to go outside. I went along with it and followed by the house rules but in my mind, I was thinking 'why would you invite me into a prison and think that I would enjoy it'? A farmhouse and a domestic townhouse have different priorities, our porch was dirty, it was where the work boots and wellies were left, the coats and overalls on the hooks could smell pungent. When town kids came to my house, I could see them staring with confusion at things that were worn and dirty. It annoyed me because I knew that they were ignorant of what a working farm really was, did they think that everybody lived in semi-detached houses with white floor tiles and cream carpets. Did they also think that all adults worked indoors and worn suits with barber trimmed hair? When they saw my father or grandfather, they were scared as if they had seen a monster. The wild curly hair and the weathered face went with the loud outdoor voice and improvised work clothes. Farmers often used old RAF leather waistcoats to keep out the rain. Sometimes they would tie paper feed bags around each leg so that they could be used and thrown away after a particularly dirty job. I found it tiresome and annoying when I saw how the town kids were perplexed. I remember at first feeling embarrassed because I knew that the town kids did not understand, but this turned into irritation, I wondered why they could not see things for what they were without being so puzzled. I myself was never so confused at the things that were unfamiliar to me, I knew it was a big world out there. Maybe the difference was that I was not brought up in a box room and not controlled so strictly, I thought that their upbringing had oppressed their development.

The town kids tended to be high maintenance, they were hard work. They were amazed that no permission was needed to eat or go outside. Given the freedom to think for themselves was liberating for such town kids and they wanted to explore, 'let's do this' and 'let's do that', they got over excited, they were a pain up the arse to me. Going in the barn or making a swing in a tree was not a new-born fascination to me as it was to them. I knew that they had been wrapped in cotton wool at home and I did not think that it had done them any good. They got scared when exploring the dark barns and when they came face to face with animals which were not in cages like at the zoo. I had to take the hoof trimming knife away because it was being yielded like a toy sword and I had to drag one boy away who was walking up behind a reversing tractor. They almost always ended up crying and hurting themselves or being in some drama one way or another. It was not because of the farm. It would be either a bee sting or an allergic reaction, or a being sick with a stomach upset. Most of the fuss was from falling over, grazes or bruises, they somehow seemed to struggle to stay upright when not on tarmac. I remember on one occasion a town kid took it on himself to start climbing a ladder, I told him to come down which he did but for some unknown reason, he jumped off the last five rungs and twisted his ankle. I remember thinking 'please go home'. When they got home, they would be reeling it all off back to their mum how they had seen a mad bull and seen poisons and potions and farm machinery. Most of them never came back, around about this same era in time, there was a public safety film about the danger on farms. It was rolled out across the country. It was shown on TV and in all the schools, it was hard-hitting, and I can remember when seeing it in my classroom, the other kids all stared at me as if I myself was a danger. After that, the event of town kids coming to my house seemed to dwindle and I was glad. The farm wasn't much of a danger to me, but it was to them, it was all down to our different upbringings. The adults on the farm did not realise how underdeveloped the town kids really were. It was wrong to assume that they had the same common sense as the farm kids, so this was a danger. The adults from the town did not seem to know anything about where they were allowing their children to go.

Once the school day had ended, returning home to the farm often saw me mucking into work before I had the chance to change my clothes, unloading straw bales or haymaking for example. There might have been cows or sheep to move about or help may have been needed to repair some broken machinery. Small hands could be a huge help, passing the spanners and the oil can or holding the torch. My clean school clothes would soon encounter smears of dirt and dust, it was as though I was being branded, back home where I belonged, I could never stay clean.

Christmas is a magical time for kids, but farm kids would often have work-hardened fathers who wouldn't acknowledge it at all, it had no part to play in the chores of the farm and helping out was expected. Leaving the festive feelings and decorations in the house for the dark and smelly cow shed to feed the corn and scape up the slurry was a stark contrast, it was a reality check. On returning to the festivities of the house, the atmosphere felt tainted, having dropped out, then back in again almost made the party look silly. As the years went on, the importance of Christmas for me declined until it was just a farse. The grown men and women who continued celebrating with vigour long after I had grown out of it was clearly in a different mindset to me. There are no regrets on my part, it was what it was, and I am all the better for it. I am glad not to be conned into the commercial drive of Christmas where there is a complete absence of religion. Easter is the same, they don't know why they rush around buying chocolate eggs and exchange them with each other, but they do. I am glad my practical upbringing has given me the sense not to follow on like a sheep.

Early in childhood, farm kids learn about the difference between pets and farm animals, we have all made the innocent mistake of befriended an animal on the farm only then to see it go to slaughter or even worse sold to someone else at the market. When that happens there is no closure and children may be left wondering if it's getting treated properly at its new home, the children would know that it was no longer a farm pet. My pig Henry was my first taste of the 'emotional switch' which the adults would use automatically. We all enjoyed Henry's playful character through that joyful summer where he grew lean. The adults knew what must be done, it was common sense to anyone apart from the young children. I suppose nothing needed to be said, we would learn what was going to happen and after all, young kids soon get over things that have gone. It was something that needed to be overcome one way or another. One day Henry disappeared and the next he was delivered back home in baskets, chopped up with his head and trotters on the top. I remember asking the man if he had suffered and I was kindly told 'no, he wouldn't have felt a thing' this would not have been far from the truth. Henry lingered in the large chest freezer for years, his head kept reappearing when we reached in for ice lollies. The head was never used it was only thrown in there for a quick job at the time of the delivery, over time it became invisible to mum who only took out what she needed whilst she was rushing around.

The cattle markets are places of business, all farm kids will have been there at one time or another. They were places of strong character accompanied by shouting and laughter. Kids would go widely ignored, it was unlike being at school where children were encouraged to speak up and the teachers would listen with interest. The children's presence in the markets was never an issue but they would rarely receive much attention, they were an irrelevance. These shrewd places of business could make for a long day for a child, this was unrealised by the parents or grandparents who had taken them there. Unknow to the adults, the children would be making observations and listening to conversations, it was a learning experience. There would be annoyed farmers unhappy with the price their stock had made and who would be asking for the opinion of others, discreetly and away from the auctioneer and the highest bidder. Others would think that they had paid too much and would be convinced that they had been deliberately run-up in the bidding. Everybody would be watching their backs, money was made when someone else had lost out. Boredom could set in and I would skulk about. Wherever I went, I always seemed to be in the way and would get bumped by big belly's in dirty checked shirts with grey chest hair sprouting out, the red faces would plough on unconcerned. As a farm kid, you would sometimes see animals from your home farm going through the ring. When they came in, the heart would instantly beat heavier and the scene would be surreal, the sight of them was so familiar, you knew the individual tufts of hair, the pattered hide or fleece and the animal's character. Time did not linger and the auctioneer would gabble away at high speed, the farm kid would look at the faces of those bidding, the underbidder looking unimpressed, the hammer would go down and they would be run out of the ring closely followed by the next lot, it made me realise that they were nothing special to anybody else, just livestock the same as the rest in the market.

Children notice the little things which adults do not, adults become blind to things that are of little significance and cease to notice them. As a child I can remember seeing all the minute details on the farm, the workshop was crammed with bits and pieces that might one day come in for some use again. There were old coco and treacle tins used to store nuts and bolts or screws. Old tobacco tins were used to contain drill bits and tyre valves. The larger tea-time biscuit tins had pictures of John Bull on them in Victorian clothes with a huge bulging stomach. The dusty tilly lamps hung up on the beams, put there thirty years ago and forgotten about. There were piles of disused cloth sacks everywhere, they had a course thread with unknown company names stencilled on the front of them. Cogs and chains were throwing about and paint tins with stains and patches on the walls where the brushes had been cleaned out. The place smelt of creosote and sawdust along with oil and grease. There was an anvil and a vice, sets of hammers, spanners and screwdrivers, all grimed up black. Propane and oxygen bottles had the welding goggles hung on the clocks with their mysterious green lenses. The grinding wheel and drill had pulleys and belts that rattled and chafed, the electric power saw was salvaged from a factory and looked like a torpedo. There was a large oil burner that glowed red when it was lit in the winter and an old boiler that filled the place with steam when it was switched on. There were electric supplies, plugs and fuses, all second had, saved and reused., coils of wire and pipe. I remember seeing and knowing all the detail as a kid but a few years later when I came to work in the shed, all these details faded away and my attention was on the job of repairing whatever it was at the time, the fascination had all gone.

The same type of observations were made in the outbuildings, old agricultural medicine bottles and things from the past that never moved for decades, milking stools and cowbells covered in house martin droppings. Old wartime gas masks and bicycles with bread baskets fitted were buried in part worn tyres and milk churns that were no longer used. The old redundant long drop toilets are too small to be of any constructive use and so things were put there that might possibly be used again or things that nobody wanted to throw away. The old farmhouse was a marvel for a detail spotting child. The ashy old range was dirty from the coal used to heat it and the kettle was black with soot. The wind whistled through making it hypnotic. The telephone was unchanged from a time when they were only black with a dial wheel and a standard ringing bell. There were black and white photographs of relatives getting married in military uniform and plant pots containing bulbs in the windowsill. A Peg rug and a rocking chair always looked so humble and simple, it was not so much old fashioned, it was more a case of being all that was needed. The large old china plates with the blue etchings were too big to be used in the kitchen so waste milk was poured in for the cats to congregate around and drink. The old barometer with its wooden frame was like the face of weather itself that presided over the living room. As a farm kid grows up, such defining details are noticed less and less. However, the smells of the farm are never forgotten, they return with as much intensity as ever, no matter how old and decrepit the body gets. A waft of newly barned hay will whisk the farmer's memory straight back to when it was first encountered. The smell of the mowing grass and the smell of the molasses used in the corn will have the same effect. There are many other examples, the smell of the silage in the winter when the air is freezing and the smell of the working dogs drying out at the fireside. I have poignant childhood memories of the harvest festivals in the church, the smell that came off the collection of fruit and vegetables was very special, it was intensified by the stale smell of the church. As we sang 'we plough the fields and scatter the good seed on the land' I would be sat in the pews staring at the glazed wheat sheaf made from bread.

Mrs Nut Case

People brought up on farms are aware of the birds and the bees from an early age. They never need "the talk" from their parents because mating is all around, the bull and the cows, the boar and the sows, the tup and the ewes. Farming is full of reproduction.

However, when it came to human courtship, farm folks could be naïve and inexperienced. I've known a few farmers that never dated, remaining tragically single for life and then dying alone. In the past, farm types would often be late in finding a partner, often in their thirties or even forties before they started dating, so many missed out on youthful courtships. It would get progressively harder for them to initiate a relationship as they got older, meaning there was an ever-increasing danger of being alone forever. I only just managed to avoid that fate myself.

Back in the day, I'd sometimes go out on the town with a couple of naïve farm lads. They had no experience with the opposite sex whatsoever, but they both wanted to find themselves a woman – they just didn't know how to go about it. They had zero social skills, and this meant it was sometimes an awkward ordeal just being with them in a pub. I was still young and still able to be kind and accommodating, but it did mean that I'd often end up in situations I didn't want to be in. A good Samaritan makes a good target, and I got more than my fair share of problem mates that nobody else would entertain.

After a few pints, the lads got their eyes on two good-looking young women standing at the bar. They stared at them shamefully, making me feel embarrassed by their socially retarded behaviour. It was clear to me that the girls were not interested; why would they want to engage with the likes of us? It wasn't that I felt they were above us; they were just town girls and they were going to be looking for a different class of conversation than the farm lads could ever offer. When it came to dating, town and country were just too far apart, the non-starters were palpable. However, it wasn't so obvious to the lads and they seemed to think they were in with a real chance. Just being in the vicinity of unknown females was almost beyond them and I had to subtly suggest that gawping wasn't a good look. The look of determination on the lads faces made them look like they might be about to grab at the women in the same way they might an escaped sheep, and I tried to explain that "pulling" women was not the same as picking out livestock in a mart.

Painfully aware of the staring, the women moved around to the other side of the bar. This should have been taken as a hint, but the lads didn't pick up on it and simply followed them. My efforts to stop them were met with, "Why don't you get off home? There's two of them and two of us." I can only imagine they thought I'd spoil their chances, and as they were never going to listen to my advice, I left them to it. I watched from the other side of the room as the women tried to avoid their advances. Conversation was never an option; they were from such different worlds that they may as well have spoken different languages. Instead, the lads started jostling up to the women and gently shoving them with their shoulders. Were they trying to initiate a relationship in some kind of primitive and animalistic way? It was like watching a tup being put to the sheep, and I wondered if there might be a sudden instinctual mounting at the bar. Thankfully, there wasn't. Luckily for the lads, the women were intelligent and kind enough to put on fake smiles and let them down gently by saying they were both engaged to be married. I doubted that very much, but the lads chose to believe it, no doubt also believing that if the women hadn't already been spoken for, they'd have been in there.

As I walked home that evening, I started to wonder if I was moving in the right social circles.

When I was in my late twenties, there was a certain woman who seemed to be readily available to anybody. She worked as a window cleaner and drove a pink van. Several old farmers had warned me about her and advised me to stay well away. I appreciated the advice, but it wasn't needed as she'd already worked her way through half the farm lads in Yorkshire and I was keeping well clear. She was of no interest to me: she was at least ten years older than me, she had five children, and her track record was shocking. She dreamed of settling down with a long-term partner, but it was evident that she was incapable of doing it. She had relationship after relationship; some only lasted a week, some only one night, and there must have been hundreds over the years. She fell out with every one of them and was spiteful and vengeful after the romances had failed. Vandalising her ex-partners vehicles in the dead of night was one of her habits, she didn't seem to realise that everyone knew that it was her who was doing it.

She'd been a bully since her school days, so her reputation spread far and wide ahead of her. She was a horrible person and had features to match. A nose like a boxer, piggy eyes, and teeth that were too small for her mouth. It was a photo-fit face of a criminal, the type you'd expect to see appear on 'Crimewatch', and I could never understand why men got involved with her. There was always gossip about who she'd just split up with (whose car had been vandalised) and who she'd now hooked up with, and I'd question how anyone could be stupid enough to go there. Some of those men must have had their brains in their trousers and absolutely nothing between their ears. Sadly, there were some sincere farm lads who fell straight into the trap. They may have genuinely wanted a relationship with someone, so it would have been an unpleasant learning experience for them when they paired up with her. I always felt smug and comfort in knowing that I would never make that mistake, however I did not get away entirely scot free.

Things I didn't want had a way of coming to me, and unbelievably, the woman moved into a house just a stone's throw away from the farm. My heart sank when I heard, and I knew what would be coming: she'd be after me. I was a single man living on my own, and she would know I was there. The fact that I'd shown no interest in her would also be annoying her, increasing her determination to make her presence known. Word came my way that she'd been asking after me and messages were being passed on to me that I was to go and see her. I did no such thing and stayed out of it. My lack of response was not appreciated. One morning, I went out to my pick-up truck and found it wrapped around in toilet roll. It was like a warning sign from the mafia. I knew who the culprit was, but the deed didn't have the desired effect and I mentioned it to no-one. She'd wanted to spark a reaction, and when it didn't come, she had to put the word out about what she'd done herself, effectively dobbing herself in to get the attention.

She was trying to indirectly create a link between herself and me, she had no shame, but I was still having none of it. I returned home from milking one morning and had just settled into my comfy chair for a snooze when I heard my front door open. A high-pitched voice called, "Hi-ya!" the syllables were lengthily drawn out. I froze. It was like a female version of Bernard had revisited. She laughingly told me it had been her that had sneaked over in the night to drape toilet roll over my vehicle (as if I didn't know) and it seemed to have been her idea of an ice-breaking prank. Considering she'd recently scratched someone's car and burnt-out a tractor, I should have considered myself lucky, but I wasn't impressed. She then proceeded to sit herself down on my lap. Not only was this unwanted, but it was also extremely awkward. She weighed a ton and she was giggling in what she must have believed was a flirty way, paying no attention to my requests for her to move. Thankfully, my mates Land Rover pulled up outside and she jumped to her feet to leave, her behaviour indicated that she was up to no good, she knew that we were a mismatch. She found my clean record annoying, her intension was to taint me with her 'been there got the T shirt' legacy. I locked the door behind her and did the same every day from then on.

She didn't return, but after a few days I started getting silent phone calls and I heard she'd been spreading rumours that I was gay. This must have been the only way she could explain my disinterest in her. The accusation was no doubt her delusional idea of revenge, but she was ignorant of the prejudice she was displaying. The rejection had clearly offended her and her need to spread the rumour persisted. Before long, she had a new man. He lasted three days and then she moved on to another two days later. It was un-Christian of me, but I couldn't help thinking that if she just started charging for her services, she'd soon be a millionaire. She appeared to have given up on me, but she had not forgotten. I woke up one morning to find all four of my tyres had been slashed. Mrs Nut Case as I now referred to her, had been drinking the entire previous day at a house party, so it didn't take Sherlock Holmes to connect the events, or so I thought.

Sadly, not everyone saw it the same way, and the imaginary battle that Mrs Nut Case had created was revealing my friends and my foes. The vandalism couldn't be proven, the gay rumours went on, and a clear rift between the wise and the stupid appeared. Perhaps the most disappointing aspect was that people chose to take sides at all. Why did people to get involved in things that had nothing to do with them? The crazy ordeal made me realise the calibre of the people around me. I'd done nothing wrong, I hadn't engaged with Mrs Nut Case, and yet I 'd suffered her trade-mark break-up wrath and vandalism. I was a decent man, and I was mortally insulted by people turning against me and supporting her. It seemed to me that people were only doing it to fuel the fire because they were relishing in my misfortune, they wanted it to last as long as it could. I used to be trusting of everyone, but this made me re-evaluate.

In addition to the other torments of farm life and my poor wages, this episode was a contributing factor in my eventual decision to change career. As I thought about it, it came to my mind that some years ago, an old farmer had given me some words of wisdom. With hindsight, I realised that he'd seen my potential and he told me, "Get yourself out of here. There's a better life for you than this." I stupidly dismissed him at the time. I didn't see or hear his wisdom; I was fooled by his appearance. He was very old, dirty and had a bushy white beard and a flat hat. I mistook him for a babbling old eccentric, but he was right. I get emotional when I think of it now. There was someone out there who could see how things were for me, but it would take me a long time before I could realise it for myself.

Bartering with Farmers

When it comes to money, farmers are tight b*ggers. I have always been known as tight, and my urban associates found my thrift absolutely hilarious. However, I thought they were reckless with their money, choosing to spend mine sensibly. I never went without anything I needed, and I saved whatever I could. People manage their money differently, and common sense is a useful asset when it comes to finances, but, once again, it's no longer so common. People spend, spend, spend as if it's a must and then complain that they have no money. On the flip side, there were some old farmers I knew that practised a whole new level of tightness that was arguably a mental illness.

I have known farmers so tight that they were unable to run their farms effectively. They wouldn't invest anything; they wouldn't buy lime to spread on the land to keep it healthy or buy any fertilizers; they'd never reseed any land or spend any money on draining it, and the land would be grazed and grazed for decades by sheep or cattle, getting progressively poorer until it could only sustain low numbers of livestock. I have seen farm buildings become so dilapidated they were beyond repair, the farmers unwilling to part with the money needed to repair them over many years. In the end, they'd be rendered useless and what was left would need to be demolished, this tightness with money creates a false economy.

There's always a need to invest money back into a business so that production and profits can be maintained rather than decline. I have known ridiculous old farmers walk around in rags simply to put off buying new clothes, and these characters could easily have been mistaken for tramps. Their wallets seemed to automatically recoil after even a few pennies found their way out, and some would consider basic needs such as soap to be an unnecessary expense. This level of scrimping was almost a disease and once it was set in, it couldn't be cured, becoming a habit and a way of life in which every decision, big or small, was based on the cost. This included eating only the cheapest of foods and doing without rather than spending money. I once overheard two such characters having a conversation at the cattle market. They were both millionaires, having inherited land and property, not to mention the scrimping they'd done over the past 60 years, but one was crying a poor tale to the other about not being able to afford supermarket prices. The other objected and pointed out that if that was the case then he wouldn't be able to afford the cigarettes he was always smoking. The first replied that if he wasn't smoking, he'd be eating, and just think how much that would cost. Can you imagine trying to barter for work with these types, as I had to?

Not all farmers were quite so bad. My family farm wasn't big enough to pay normal wages, so I topped up my money by being self-employed and working on other farms. This was convenient in that I could choose when I wanted the extra work, it was very flexible, but the downside was trying to get paid. I learned which farmers to work for and which to give a wide berth. Some farmers would be accustomed to paying staff and knew that there was no way around it, realising that if they wanted to keep good employees, they'd need to pay good rates. I have no doubt most of them learned this the hard way, having previously been gas-tight and wondering why good workers never came back. I eventually accumulated enough regular employers to never be short of work but getting there was a steep and painful learning curve.

Many farmers were not fit to do business with. These were often the ones who'd rarely employed anyone and seemed to think that grown men would work for a pittance. I was caught out many times, I was naïve, and I struggled to barter with them. I had to try to make them see sense and I'd lay out all my expenses in full to help them understand that I wasn't trying to rob them. Firstly, there was the cost of the diesel fuel to get me there and back each day, and then there was the cost of my lunch, not to mention the cost of the breakfast that I'd be working on until lunchtime, effectively making it a cost incurred. I'd have to explain to the farmer that on top of this, I also wanted to make some profit, pointing out that I could just sit at home all day for nothing rather than ragging my arse out for the same. We'd eventually compromise and settle on the minimum wage, but the farmer was often showing signs of shock by this point. Before long, I learned not to bother trying to explain why I needed to be paid properly, I just gave them a price. If they started arguing the toss, then it was a clear sign to walk away.

Repairing dry-stone walls was one of my specialities. It's hard work, but if a farmer has fallen walls all over a property it looks terrible. Even small gaps can have a ton of stone in them, and this all needs to be repaired from the bottom up so there's digging to be done with a pick and shovel at the base before reassembling can begin. I went to one farm where the walls looked like they'd been blitzed by torpedoes, and at least twenty gaps were visible to anyone passing by. I repaired the lot and people would often say to me that I'd literally repaired the landscape as it looked a million times better than it did before. Work like this always brought me more offers of work as the results of my efforts could be clearly seen. The workmanship seemed to please everyone – except the farmer. He wasn't quite so over the moon and had probably spent the last couple of weeks on tenterhooks worrying about having to pay for the work. When I went to get paid, he was nowhere to be found.

He was no doubt hiding away somewhere, quite possibly the hen hut, stewing and sweating over any excuse he could conjure up to justify a discount. When I eventually caught up with him, the hesitations over the payment would begin with a commonly heard phrase, "Can you take any less?" I'd sometimes lose a snip just to get done with the job and get any kind of payment, but these characters made me sick.

Sometimes I'd work a week or two on a job and the farmer would say something like, "It hasn't taken you long." This would be his way of implying that it should be cheaper because it seemed to be a quick job, and I think they were perhaps disappointed that I hadn't had to suffer for longer to merit the price agreed. I learned to have answers ready for the tight-fisted queries these misers came up with. It was usually the case that a dry-stone wall repair was never straight forward. Extra stone would be needed, and it would always be found in a pile in a distant field corner. This had to be collected and transported using my own vehicle, and I'd quickly point out that this was extra work I hadn't charged for. The suggestion that I could ask to be paid more, not take less, was often all it took for them to swiftly settle on the original price. They no doubt felt vindicated that at least some of the work I'd done had been done for nothing.

There was one old b*gger that refused to pay me anything at all at the end of a job. I'd repaired a gap in his wall, but his refusal to pay was because (according to him) I'd used the best stone from his pile. I'd dug a metre deep into a bog to find a solid foundation for that wall and hurt my back in the process – and all for nothing. I never worked for him ever again, and I waited ten years before I went back and kicked that wall down in the middle of the night. These experiences hardened my attitudes, all naivety was smashed out of me, and I soon learned to be no one's fool. I could smell a rat a mile off and I became suspicious of any new clients that approached me. Why would they need to come looking for me if there was a good job up for grabs? One old farmer approached me about repairing his walls. He said he had a lot of walls down, but he didn't have much money. I didn't barter. I simply replied, "Well, you'd better leave your walls down then," before walking away.

On another occasion, I was approached with a blinder of a proposition. A farmer was having lorry deliveries numerous times per week, and they were coming 50 miles up the A1 each time. He proposed that I did the haulage with his tractor and trailer to save him money. All well and good, but, his old tractor and trailer were nothing short of dangerous and he'd worked out, factoring in the diesel costs, that he could pay me two pounds per hour. He must have begrudged paying what was clearly a fair price for the professional haulage and had come up with the idea of getting me to do it for less. No way was I going to risk my life and endanger the lives of others in a dangerous vehicle that was entirely inappropriate for the job or the journey. It was insulting that he'd even asked me: did he think I was so poverty-stricken that I'd accept an offer like that? I stared him in the eye and angrily told him to get lost – or words to that effect. He must have realised he'd misjudged me and that his sly old b*st**d tricks were not going to work as he looked away and scurried off back to his fox hole, defeated. Of course, like all other old b*gger farmers, he wasn't offended. He was only concerned with his own business and not at all concerned by my anger, he was just looking for someone to do it. The scary thing is, he probably found some young naïve lad to do it. They wouldn't be bothered by the low pay, they'd only be interested in driving the tractor. All I can say is that whoever ended up doing it, they were unfit to do the job because anyone with any sense would have said no. The next time you hear about a farm accident, just bear in mind that it may well have been caused by this type of cost-cutting in some way or form.

Understanding the Farmer

The term "farmer" is loosely used. Some employed farmworkers call themselves farmers whilst others are referred to as farmers and they will disapprove of it. I have no complaint either way. The farmers which I refer to in this book are the hard life types who were born into it. I do not write about gentleman or landlord farmers, or the romantics who draw attention to how lovely their farm is. I write about the ones in overalls and ragged overcoats who dressed for necessity and who were dirty from work, they would normally have a pained look on their face.

Obviously not all farmers are the same. They have moderately evolved since the days which I write about and I'd say that the modern-day farmer is much less distinctive. That said, it's still possible to identify the more extreme cases simply by looking at them in the street. They look lost and bewildered when visiting the town; they're out of their comfort zone and probably visiting the bank or paying bills which they will not be enjoying. It's like the classic children's story of the town mouse and the country mouse. The town mouse is out of his depth in the countryside and likewise the country mouse in the town.

The stereotypical image of a farmer is someone with a weathered and enlarged red face, a big nose, probably a mass of curly hair, and perhaps a few missing teeth. They usually have a limp or move very stiffly, as though carrying an invisible sack of potatoes on their back, tell-tale signs of prolonged hard labour. In reality, you might not meet such an image, but today's farmers can still stand out simply because of their somewhat warped dress sense. This is especially true if they're not wearing work clothes and they're trying to look smart. I know this from first-hand experience. My dress sense was decidedly warped and no matter how hard I tried to look normal, I was fighting a losing battle. Of course, much of this can be blamed on me spending so much of my time alone. I had enough to worry about without concerning myself with my appearance and I never took notice of what other people were wearing. There was a time when I'd wear corduroy trousers on a night out, thinking they were smart. I had no concept of the fact that they were widely laughed at. There must have been many occasions on which I unwittingly dressed like a complete buffoon. I attended wedding parties wearing big yellow woolly jumpers and beige loafers. I found it annoying that people stared at me, but I remained oblivious as to why. It would be years later before the extent of my fashion faux pas would become clear to me. Farmers work alone and thereby they learn to live by their own decisions; they're not easily influenced. I did wonder why people kept giving me their old clothes. I think they must have been trying to subtly influence my dress sense, but I never twigged at the time. These days, I stick to wearing work clothes, and I keep a clean set for going into town.

Farmers can be identified by the vehicle they drive. This will almost certainly be a four-wheel drive and virtually guaranteed to have copious amounts of dried mud splashed up every side. A small area on the windscreen will have been scraped clean by the wiper, and the same on the rear window, which may account for the slow speeds these vehicles are driven at, but it may also be down to the amount of time spent driving tractors. If you're unlucky enough to get stuck behind such a vehicle on the road, you'll no doubt discover that overtaking is not an easy option as they tend to randomly drift across the white lines. This is due to gawking at other people's fields as they drive along. Bumps and dings will also be in evidence all over the bodywork and bumpers, and the indicators will not be working – or is it that they're just not being used? All in all, these vehicles send out a strong message: there's no place for vanity in this driver's life and they are only concerned with their own business. This farmer is not trying to impress anyone.

Should you ever be inside one of these vehicles, you'll be met with a distinct aroma of animals, accompanied by the sight of sh*t smeared all around the footwells. Rubbish and paperwork will be randomly scattered along the dash and over the passenger seat. There may be animal medicines in a variety of bottles and syringes along with feed buckets and corn bags in the back, and you're more than likely to find a highly alert working-dog sitting amongst it all, keeping watch over the vehicle as it waits for their owner's return. The wait is rarely a long one as a visit to the town is kept as brief as possible.

The farmer can be difficult to approach, making him or her appear cold, or even ignorant. They can come across as dismissive and suspicious, even hateful, and ruthlessly blunt to the point of being belittling. I have been on the receiving end of it and, later in life, I would be the one dishing it out. I now understand the reasons why, and it's these reasons I hope to explain.

Someone born and brought up on a working farm has it in their blood. Their unique learning and understanding of this life will have begun long before they ever realised. They would witness birth and death on their doorstep when they're toddlers. They'll have see unsuccessful calvings, cows that are in pain and then dead calfs; they'll see the death rate in pig litters and the runt being rejected, sometimes even bitten in half by the sow, and they'll see frail new-born lambs brought into the kitchen in an effort to warm them up, only for most of them to eventually die. Young children get used to helping out as soon as they're able, perhaps taking on the task of collecting hen eggs from the nesting boxes as a first job. Such little tasks are a pleasure and helping out becomes natural. As the years go on, a child becomes handier and they're unwittingly working on the farm without knowing any different. A vast variety of skills will become second nature to these youngsters and by high school age, they are a jack-of-all-trades. The farm teaches plumbing and electrics, carpentry and mechanics, building, horticulture, and agriculture. Tools can be used impressively, vehicles of every description can be driven, and, as farming is business, an understanding of economics is inherent.

When I was still a schoolboy, I'd occasionally end up working with young men around ten years my senior. They'd be in their first job and probably still finding their feet, and they may have come to the farm working on a contract or to deliver and assemble some new equipment. As they were my seniors, I'd always assume they were skilled and would teach me something. I increasingly found that I was more skilled than most of them and I'd end up taking the lead myself. I'd been gaining experience since I was a toddler, and them only since they had left school. They'd give up on jobs, saying it was impossible or that heavy machinery was needed, but I'd just quietly carry on and show them that most of the time all that was needed to make progress was determination. When the job was complete, they'd be amazed, and it provided a tale for them to tell.

My upbringing had made me a proficient worker. When I was 15, I had to do 'Work Experience' through the school. I didn't understand the concept, so a teacher explained to me that this was to gain experience of work. I couldn't believe it. Until that point, I hadn't considered that other children at school had done nothing other than be children. They'd been treated and looked after like children, and when they weren't at school, they were playing. It made me consider the differences between them and myself. For a start, most of the other lads had pearl-white hands and fingernails while mine looked like the hands of an old fisherman, callused and dirty, and I never could get the dirt out from under my fingernails. Their lives had been so different compared to mine, and it was no wonder they were so immature by comparison. I had an old head on my shoulders, and I didn't talk unnecessarily or joke around that much. I had a serious, slightly worried look on my face as a kid, whereas the other kids had faces like bouncing babies, all wide-eyed as they smiled and laughed at everything. Of course, the other kids had learned social skills from an early age, playing together in the park and going to each other's houses. Farm kids hadn't. They would be absent from these meetings as there would be pressing issues back on the farm. The disparity between us became more obvious as time went on. I was socially inferior, but at least I was a seasoned worker. This stuck with me throughout my life and I began to assume that wherever I was working, I'd be the superior worker. It wasn't always the case, and I never failed to be impressed whenever I wasn't.

There's a widespread misconception that you never see a poor farmer. This is incorrect. Wealth can vary hugely across the industry. At the top of the wealth pile, there are royal farmers. The aristocrat farmer operates predominantly through tradition, a rich man's hobby if you like. The title of the farmer is proudly worn by these types, but all the real work is undertaken by staff. These days, upper-class farming seems to involve the conservation of rare breeds, providing little or no financial reward, and environmental projects such as laying hawthorn hedges have become the trend.

Some affluent farmers own and work thousands of acres of land. Their businesses are well established and successful, having been grown over many generations, and they seldom go wrong whatever they do. However, further down the pile are those who farm in poverty. Some will rent smallholdings and run them at a loss, but these types of farmers wouldn't have it any other way. It's a way of life that they desire, and they will continue to stick with it no matter what. It's on a parallel with the aristocrat farmer, only this is a poor man's hobby. Neither one makes any money out of farming, yet one is admired and the other is generally condemned as a nut case.

Farmers habitually live in bubbles. This is inevitable. They are self-employed, and they carry all responsibility on their own. It's hard work, there's no real guidance or help in terms of knowing how to operate a farm, and there's no shortage of pitfalls. There is, however, a list of regulatory bodies and people that could step in and change things at any point. The inland revenue, for example. They can investigate businesses at random and may find some costly error in the accounts. Changes in legislation are always pending, and this could be detrimental if demanding specific changes that could reduce the farm's profits. There are no set prices for the product and there are penalties imposed by the buyers where vegetables or livestock are overgrown. There are certificates and paperwork that go with the livestock, and if any of these are incorrect, it may result in an animal being discarded into the waste at the slaughterhouse and no payment received. There are always looming disease pandemics that could wipe out a farm's entire livestock, and there is a constant threat of theft hanging over most farms. When machinery is stolen, it can wipe out a year's earnings, even when insured. All manner of fines and prosecutions can pop up unexpectedly. Accidents are not uncommon in the farming industry, and police or health and safety investigations could yield crippling fines or even prison sentences for the farmer if found to be negligent. Environmentalists and animal rights activists are always trying their best to find violations and make damming reports, and the farmer must take responsibility for all of this. He or she will have all of this on their mind as they make decisions over what to invest their time and effort into each year, effectively taking one financial gamble after another. It's a far cry from working in the public sector, where income is guaranteed, welfare and working conditions are the finest, trade unions automatically fight to make things even better, and where lump-sum pay-outs and early retirements with hefty pensions seem to be awarded even after years of taking it comparatively easy, sick pay is available when feeling stressed – no questions asked.

On top of this, farmers always have a long list of jobs that need to be done in addition to their daily duties. Some of these will have been pending for years and he or she will never know if they're ever likely to get done. They tend to be large jobs that need a build-up of guts and determination to tackle. Jobs such as taking a barn roof off and renewing it or replacing a kilometre of fencing across the fields. Materials deteriorate over the years and need to be replaced, meaning many of these big jobs will already have been done at least once before by the farmer. There are always things to be done in mind: rewiring buildings, repairing roads and lanes, and gateways are constantly needing to be widened to accommodate changing machinery. Once upon a time they were eight feet wide, then they were ten, and now they're twelve or fifteen. These endless missions must be timed to coincide with relatively quiet times of the year. This might be in between putting the fertiliser on and mowing the grass, or after the harvest but before the winter. The farmer learns how to operate while carrying this heavy load on the mind, the casual farm labourer is often unaware of it.

Living in bubbles can make people different. I've seen many farming families effectively closed off from the outside world, they develop unique little ways and behaviours. This happens when there's nothing else to compare with, and these little ways can look very strange to someone coming in from the outside. On many of these old-fashioned family farms, hard-working farmers and their wives would work on into their old age alongside their children. The children could be in their fifties, but their parents would still be in charge. Farming can hold the family unit together for decades, and it can be a pleasant way of life, but the bubble effect can also incubate illogical practices.

I once knew a farm like this. It was a simple pig farm and the place was a mess, but the family didn't know it. They were squirrelling away scrap metal and it had long since gotten out of hand. Most farms keep their scrap metal until there's a big enough pile to warrant cashing it in, but this farm had scrap in every cavity and corner. Anything metal was saved. This included old machinery, washing machines, wrecked cars, biscuit tins and even a pile of used tin foil. The scrap was corroding because it was so old, but the farmer was obsessed with it and constantly feared it would get stolen. This obsession had passed onto his sons. They were stuck in a rut of collecting and keeping scrap and then worrying about it getting stolen. It did have a value, but it wasn't worth worrying about. The subject came up one day when I was talking to the sons, so I decided to put them straight on it. I told them the scrap was worth a few hundred pounds at most, and they could get rid of it by getting it weighed at the scrap yard. They looked at me in disbelief, as if I'd insulted them and disrespected their father. However, they thought about it and a week later they took it all to the scrap yard. My advice was so far removed from what they knew and the way they did things that it was hard to comprehend initially, but it had been accepted. The situation needed some intervention. Fresh eyes were needed to point out the obvious things that they'd become blind to. The piles of scrap had almost become part of the furniture, and the collection and protection of it were far outweighing its actual purpose. It should have been cashed in long ago, but they were so locked into their ways that they couldn't see the wood for the trees.

I found another little family farm bubble one day when I went to a farm with a lorry to pick up a load of pigs. The abode had no immediate neighbours and it was down a long, unmade road. There was no loading ramp and I couldn't reverse up to the pig shed because of scattered farm implements and yard clutter. The farmer, his wife, and their young daughter were on hand to assist, plus a yappy little Jack Russell dog. A gantry had to be fashioned out of old pallets, knackered gates, bits of wood, and a few barrels to block up the gaps, and the plan was to send the pigs out of the shed and down into the lorry: what could go wrong? The farmer went into the shed to send the pigs out, but after ten minutes, they still hadn't appeared. This gave me a heads up that I was in for an ordeal. Eventually, the pigs started sniffing their way out apprehensively, and it became apparent that they'd never left the shed until now. They'd have been born in there and then fattened up in there, and they were going to be obstinate. They started routing and poking at the makeshift gantry which instantly began falling to bits. Pigs were escaping and had to be rounded up, and any that made it down to the lorry door had to be shoved on by hand, only to then turn around and walk straight back out again. Tensions and frustrations started to show.

The farmer began to shout and scream at his wife, aiming all his anger at her, blaming her alone for all that was happening. The farmer's wife, in turn, was firing all her anger solely at their daughter, blaming her for the situation, and the daughter was laying all her anger into the dog, blaming it for yapping and scaring the pigs. It had clearly become a hierarchical blame game, and I don't think any one of them knew they were doing it, but it was vicious and relentless. I, on the other hand, was treated like royalty by all of them. I was an unfamiliar face, so I was excluded from the fault-finding, and even when a pig managed to slip past me, someone else got the blame.

This torment continued for some time until I also began losing my rag. Up until that point, I'd been too polite to say anything, it was their farm after all. I got sick of hearing all the blaming, it had no constructive use whatsoever, and I started to point out the real problems: "It's not her fault, the pallet is falling to bits," and, "Your wife isn't strong enough to shove them in, why don't you do it?" Direction was needed, so I told the daughter to shut the dog away and told the farmer to let the daughter have the easier position. They were instantly submissive, doing everything I said, and I found it rather strange. It was as though they looked up to me, even though they'd only just met me, but they looked down on each other.

When the lorry was loaded, we were all red in the face, dripping with sweat, and covered in pig sh*t. We began to smile at each other and snigger. We'd done it, even though it had been a nightmare and we'd all descended into rollicking one another. I made a kind of Churchillian speech at that point, telling them that playing the blame game wasn't constructive, but getting new gates and improving the set up would be. They were stuck in their blaming routine and unable to think outside of it. It took someone new to point out the obvious. Unless they changed, nothing would change. Having a "stranger" there had forced them to step out of their bubble.

Stale thinking on these places was an occupational hazard. It can develop anywhere that the pace of life is slow and repetitive, and where nothing much ever changes. In such environments, the old-fashioned ways linger longer than usual, and independent thinking can be something that only catches up relatively late in life. Understanding things like this requires open and intelligent thought, but people looking in from the outside tend to just write it off as weird, simply because it's something they're unfamiliar with.

I've often been around people having conversations about how strange farmers are. They wouldn't know that I was a farmer, and I wouldn't bother to tell them. There was no simple conversation that could have disentangled the misunderstandings, and I knew that they'd have no interest in a lengthy debate. I had learned that sometimes things are best left alone, and there would be no benefit in trying to educate them.

Weird or wonderful comes down to a person's point of view. These self-contained farms could be heavenly, and it was in such places that I often met the happiest and most contented people. Today, highly successful and affluent individuals from the cities often spend their money trying to create such a place – a quiet place to bring up a family and grow their own food. Some see this as an ideal way of life, not a weird or a poor way of life. The beauty is always in the eye of the beholder, some can see it, others can't.

Farmers need to be driven individuals, and it can feel like a constant battle as the farm tries to break them with challenge upon challenge. They develop a thick skin and they fight on, irrespective of the poor living, and the fight becomes a way of life; all-consuming. It's a bit like the famous story of Captain Ahab in Moby Dick and how his obsession with the white whale leads to him being taken down with it. Farming is a lifelong obsession unless you give up, but once it's in someone's blood, they don't give up. That's why 80-year-old farmers struggle on. They fear giving up because if they no longer farm, what are they? An empty shell. Being a farmer makes them different.

I was born into a working farm of 50 sheep and 50 cows, plus poultry, pigs, and contracting work, but it didn't yield a high enough income, so I also worked on other farms. In my twenties, I managed to attend what was billed as a full-time course at a local university, but there was so much free time that I continued to work almost without interruption. Later in life, I took a job in a large utility company and progressed into a good position, I still continued to work on the farm at home. By this time, I was no longer burdening myself with work on other farms, so I was no longer having to cope with lunatic farmworkers. Doing a degree course meant that I could now earn an easy income, and I didn't have to worry about not being as young and fit as I once was. The experiences I'd had made me painfully aware of the huge differences between farm life and urban life, and these differences continued to be difficult to deal with. To say the two are worlds apart is an understatement. There's a huge gap to bridge, but it's not one that everyone needs to cross, and some will never even know it's there.

The abyss between farmers and townsfolk is often downplayed, but it can ruin friendships, relationships, and marriages. The weight of this problem is always being carried by the farmer who must try to juggle time and unforeseeable events with a third party who has no comprehension of the difficulty. Pencilling in social events on the calendar is always a risky thing to do and farmers do not like to do it. They don't like doing it simply because they can't be sure of what will happen on any given day and therefore can't guarantee they'll be able to honour the pencilled in arrangement. Birthdays during harvest time might be a good example. If the crop is ready and dry, it needs to be reaped, and leaving it until tomorrow when it might rain is too great a risk to take. Getting the crop in has financial value, attending a party has not.

This is the farmer's income, his livelihood, but when cancellations are regular occurrences, friends or partners can't always understand the reason. If they don't understand farming, patience can wear thin and reasons for not attending can begin to be seen as excuses, and not necessarily believed. Townsfolk working in nine to five jobs have no concept of these seasonal constraints. When farmers are invited to attend social events, they hope to be able to join in, but whatever the event, it will need to fit in around the on-going farm work that will always take precedence. For this reason, farmers are rarely the organisers of social events, they wait to be invited, but when they've had to cancel a time or two, the invites often stop. When the invitations stop, it all stops. There's a strange irony to this in that the third party never seems to take the time to think about the reasons behind last-minute cancellations or to understand the challenges faced by the farmer in question. If the tables were turned, they might finally see things differently. Imagine if their boss announced at lunchtime that they had to get a report completed and onto his desk by the end of the day or they'd lose half of their annual salary... I don't think they'd be out drinking at a barbeque all afternoon. This imaginary scenario is unlikely to ever happen, but it hammers home the point that in a farmer's world, there's no contest. Their livelihood must always come first.

Many moons ago, an old college friend rang to say that he was about to set off and he was on his way over to me for our planned night out. This had been planned some time ago, but other happenings had pushed it out of my mind. It was a warm and sunny friday night, the start of what promised to be a sunny Bank Holiday weekend, and my old friend must have thought it was a perfect evening for beer-swilling. However, I had ten acres of hay that had dried out in record time and was ready to bale. It could have normally needed a few more days, but it was perfection as it was, and leaving it meant risking a morning dew that could quickly lead into a nosedive in quality. The sun is not guaranteed to come through the next day. Getting it at its best meant getting it baled right away as weather forecasts couldn't be relied upon.

The baled hay would fill the barn and good quality hay could be sold at a premium. If there's an abundance of hay in a good year and there is a surplus, it can be used to feed cattle or sheep. Dairy cows will produce milk on good hay and sheep will only eat good hay. A barn full of poor hay can't be sold, nobody wants it, cows won't do well on it, and sheep won't eat it. The difference between premium quality and poor quality all hinged on that friday night. I took the time to explain all of this to my friend on the phone, making sure he understood the reason for such a short-notice cancellation, but he didn't get it. He said, "Why does it have to be done tonight? Just leave it." The gap of understanding was too great to bridge. I could have gone on to explain to him that other family members had already started preparing the barn, the hay was being rowed up ready for the tractor and baler, the trailers were coupled up, and the loader tractor was getting refuelled, so where did me going out to swill some beer fit into this, but it would have fallen on deaf ears. He wouldn't and perhaps simply couldn't understand it. Our meetings became more infrequent after that until they eventually stopped.

Another friend of mine liked to have a big party every year on his birthday. I was always invited but, unfortunately, it fell in the middle of harvest time. I only ever managed to attend two of these parties over 20 years of being invited, and on those occasions, it was only because it was piddling rain and all work had to stop.

When a cancellation isn't required, other obstacles can more or less guarantee that a farmer will be late to an occasion. Such obstacles might be helping a cow to calf, restoring the livestock's water supply after a pump has failed, or fixing a puncture. If you count the number of tyres being used on a typical farm, you can rapidly get to one hundred plus. All of these carry the risk of punctures or blowouts, and they'll invariably happen just as the day is almost done. They can't be left because the vehicle will be needed first thing in the morning, so fixing them is going to make you late. These happenings can make life awkward if you're dating and your date doesn't understand farming. Things get even worse if your date's parents become aware of these incidents, and your repeated failure to arrive at social events on time can have them brand you as a rear-end (or words to that effect,) seeing you as unreliable or even dysfunctional, looking at you in a way that suggests they're thinking the only possible explanation for your behaviour is drug addiction. This complete lack of understanding is both infuriating and insulting. The farmer can see and understand both sides of the predicament, but the other parties tend to only see their own.

This begs the question of whether a relationship between a farmer and a non-farmer can ever work. Whether the farmer is a man or a woman, the person they settle down with can't be needy, or the relationship is doomed to fail. In the case of a farmer's wife, for example, if she's adaptable and hardworking herself, and mature enough to deal with the disappointments that the farm life demands, then she'll have little difficulty staying the course. They must have what it takes to pick up and carry on, particularly so when children come along because an imbalance in childcare responsibilities is par for the course. Outdoors work on the farm never stops. I have seen farms slowly poison marriages until they die a frustrating death. The farmer may realise that their level of absence is killing the relationship, but they can't do anything about it. They're torn in half; they are trying to do one thing as the other cries out for help. I would always advise prospective farm wives or husbands to run a long trial period when dating, maybe several years.

Some non-farming partners proclaim that they love the farming life, but their imaginings of what it entails may have been derived from television, in which case they're going to be disappointed. Initial interest is all well and good, staying up late harvesting with your new farmer partner on a warm pleasant evening in the early stages of dating can feel like a romantic adventure, but this is just the pre-marriage honeymoon period. The farmer will try harder than ever before to fit things in and will take calculated risks to go courting, stealing time away from the farm. However, these stolen moments eventually come back to bite. It always seems to be the case that things go wrong on the very day a farmer takes time off. A day trip to the seaside will be the day an animal gets its head stuck in a gate or the day that floods, power cuts, or some other disaster will present. These things are costly, and the temptation to venture out soon wanes, especially as the farmer's guilt grows. The newfound novelty of farming life will wear off for the newcomer, and the farm will become the third entity in the relationship. Jealousy and resentment creep in.

It can, of course, work with the right person. There's no room for airs and graces or vanity, and they need to be realistic, with no airy-fairy aspirations or ambitions that are too far removed from the farm. An attitude of make do and mend is needed, along with patience to wait for everything. These are not childlike qualities, they require maturity, so it's inconvenient that most pairing up takes place when both parties are young. I've seen a few whirlwind romances between farmers and whatever you call the opposite of a farmer, and these would quickly lead into marriage. Opposites attract. Some impressive individuals survive the shock to the system and adapt to make it work, but others drift apart and separate. I knew a farmer who lived on a remote little dump of a farm where he milked cows. The place looked half derelict and the yard was deep in slop, the house itself little more than a converted cow shed. His new wife was a nurse. She was a (bottle) blonde and she was never seen without a thick layer of makeup, making it appear very much a mismatch – heaven only knows how they got through the dating phase. The house stank of sour milk, a smell that clings to the clothes of anyone milking cows, but once she moved in, things began to change. The house interior was painted in bright designer colours, modern blinds went up in the windows, a bright yellow patio and car parking space appeared outside the door, and glazed plant pots with little shaped bushes were placed on the corners. It was a nice effort, but it was representational of the relationship. The décor was typical of a trendy newbuild house in a town housing estate, but this is not what this house was. It was an old, worn down, and dirty habitat. The very essence of the place was farming. It stood on its own on a hillside and it looked like a toil of a residence. The fact that the farm was still there was living proof that the people who ran it were determined survivors and must be committed to the life.

There were no neighbours to chat with, and no one to see the glammed-up living quarters. The farmer never had visitors as he'd isolated himself years ago. In his mind, this was the most convenient thing to do as pals eventually fall out of favour and become inconveniences. The new wife was accustomed to inviting friends over for dinner and drinks and she tried to continue this lifestyle in her new abode, but the setting didn't fit. Guests would arrive all dressed up and made up, carrying bottles of wine, the taxi drivers having struggled to find the place and then getting stuck in the mud. I often wondered if such places would ever have been filled with the sounds and smells of a party before, the yard now full of the aroma of exotic perfumes. Drinks would be served inside as the farmer finished up the milking outside, and then he'd be greeted by visibly shocked faces as he came in wearing dirty overalls, overpowering all other perfumes with his pungent smell. This clears up any mistaken ideas about this little place out in the sticks being a style gimmick.

After a quick wash and change, the farmer then joins the party and tries to interact, but it's hard when conversations revolve around the colourful lives, past and present, of the visitors. Small-talk subjects such as films, fashion, or sport are all aspects of life that have generally passed him by and he has little to say, so questions will be sympathetically asked by the visitors to give him an opportunity to speak. These questions will be along the lines of, "How many cows do you have?" or, "Have you always lived on the farm?" but there's no genuine interest in hearing the answers. A naïve or drunk farmer may go into detail, describing all the ins and outs of the job, but the pretence of interest can only last for so long. Eyes will begin to glaze over, and the fixed smiles on faces will falter as people look for an excuse to escape. A more clued-up farmer would just give a quick one-line answer to honour the conversion attempt, allowing the asker to move on. Not everyone can have something in common with everyone else, and farm-folk meeting townsfolk is a classic example. After the meal, the farmer would begin to look at the clock, wondering how late the guests intend to stay. He has an early start in the morning, whereas everyone else in the room is probably intending to sleep off a hangover until at least noon. The drinks keep flowing well past midnight, but the farmer has already made his apologies and gone to bed, alienating him even more.

Soon enough, the social events would be held in restaurants and bars instead. This made things easier to organise as well as making it easier to conclude the night at a reasonable hour. The only problem with this arrangement would be the farmer running late when something cropped up, or perhaps not being able to go at all, leaving the spouse to go alone. These get-togethers would be a reminder of her former, much more enjoyable, carefree life, and doubts would begin to creep in. Returning home to the isolated workaholic partner would provide a stark contrast.

I knew what this farmer's house was like before he got married. It was typical of a farmer living in a self-sufficient world. There were no ornamental trimmings, everything in the place had a practical use and cleaning was confined to the kitchen sink and bathroom only. There were waist-high piles of newspapers, often donated by other people, as old newspapers are good for lighting fires, soaking up spillages, insulating poultry crates, or even browsing through occasionally. They were kept, piled up, and saved, but his new wife would no doubt have seen all of this as rubbish and cleared it away. The sheepdog used to have an old sofa chair in the kitchen. It was shiny with grime and covered in hairs, but it never seemed to get any worse. The relationship with the dog used to bring contentment and happiness, but after the marriage, it had to be kept outside in a shed. The kitchen used to be simple and old-fashioned. There was a modest square table that always had a checked tablecloth on it with a butter dish, vinegar bottle, and salt and pepper pots. The stove had a whistling kettle, and there was a radio next to the bread bin, but other than the peg rug, that was about it. The farmer didn't realise how perfect this was for the life he lived, or how inconsiderate his wife was being by removing it and replacing it with fixtures and fittings that made the place look like a show booth in a homeware store.

The wife tried to play out her normality, while the farmer tried to bend over backwards to do it with her. When the holiday season came around (an alien concept to most farmers) there was a mad dash to book a holiday and get him a passport. In his desperation, he harvested early, rushing to make it fit in with the holiday dates. As always, there would be a penalty to pay somewhere along the line. Someone had to be employed to run the farm while they were away, and this was a big risk as mistakes could be made, but the farmer braced himself and committed to getting away. It all proved to be more trouble than it was worth for him, especially as the holiday took him completely out of his comfort zone. Going on holiday is a thing that farmers rarely did. A "holiday" for most was a day trip to the seaside and even then, work was never far from their minds. They always brought back a seaside novelty straw hat as these are ideal for keeping the sun off the neck when working on the hay.

A couple of years later, the pair had a baby. I was on the farm helping to get the grass into the silage pit that year and it was all hands-on deck with three tractors and trailers working to bring the grass in, sort it, and roll it down into the pit. The farmer himself was in the field on the forager that blows the grass into the trailers. The operation was in full swing, it was the first day of harvesting, and it was looking good when the farmer suddenly started heading back to the farm. Everyone assumed there must be some kind of mechanical issue with the forager, but instead, he announced with some embarrassment that he'd have to call it a day because he had to go with his wife to have the baby photographs taken. I doubt very much that this was his idea and all of us were left slightly gobsmacked by this turn of events. Could it be that he was pandering to her rather than her adapting or compromising to fit in with farm work? As it was, I had other work commitments for the rest of the week and couldn't go back, and the other lads refused to go back as they'd expected to work and be paid for a full 12 hours that day, not two. I have no idea how he finished the silage that year.

As time went on, the invisible divide between them finally split them apart. His house reverted to the comforts of before, the dog moved back in, and the wife was never seen there again. The fancy plants died, and the pots grew a covering of moss, making them finally blend in. I can only assume that she took him for half of the farm and that he had to put it on a mortgage to keep it. The marriage was a casualty of the gap of understanding, painfully demonstrating that some people can never get past it. The farmer went on into old age milking the cows and he stayed on his own for the rest of his life. Sad as it seems, I think he was glad to do so.

Once the chaos of trying to please unfamiliar people is over, it's not something that's likely to be repeated. When a farmer settles into where he belongs, he doesn't want a life disturbed by others. This might seem selfish as they only go where they want, and do what they want when they want, but it's the only way it can work. Trying to do otherwise will only ever end in disappointment and resentment. Farmers learn not to stress themselves out trying to accommodate those who do not understand, choosing to cut them off dead and leave them to their own ends. In the end, this is much healthier than trying to juggle the impossible.

One such impossible situation can occur at lambing time. A farmer lambing 300 sheep needs to give them round the clock supervision. Many births need assistance, some lambs will need to be bottle-fed, and new-born lambs need to have their navels sprayed with iodine to stop infections getting in. The lambing shed needs to be mucked out constantly and replenished with fresh bedding and water, and sheep need to be moved about and organised on an on-going basis. It's a vital time on the farm and the farmer's performance will be reflected in his bank balance. Now, imagine at this crucial time, some townie acquaintance from high school pesters the farmer to attend their birthday party. This is not a children's party, it's a middle-aged party, but they're having balloons and birthday cake, and they want everyone there to sing "Happy Birthday". It's hard for the farmer to understand why a grown-up feels the need to have such a party, having grown out of such events around the age of ten and seeing it as embarrassingly self-absorbed and pathetic, but he's unable to attend anyway – it's lambing time. His failure to attend leads to black looks and it becomes clear that it was taken personally and treated like a snub. What else can the farmer do when faced with such impossibilities but turn his back on the lot of them and make sure he's never asked again. It makes life much simpler.

Livestock auction markets are places where farmers can socialise with other farmers, safe havens away from ridiculous people with no common sense – but not always. Farmers get so sick of the gap of understanding that they'll tend to avoid non-farmers altogether and if they're approached by a stranger, especially an urban stranger, they're quick to put up their guard. This comes from experience. Farmers live in a self-sufficient world, so what benefit can anyone approaching them possibly bring? It could be someone selling insurance, or equipment on commission. It might be someone wanting to store something on the farm, or wanting to buy land at a knockdown price, or tip rubble as a cheap way of getting rid of it. Sometimes it's a job enquiry or work experience request, and I've even had people approach me about wanting to make a football pitch in the field. Someone once asked, "Could I try driving a tractor?" so any suggestion of wanting to build houses on the land leaves me cold. Why would I want more ridiculous people on my doorstep?

Serious farmers seldom have hobbies. The fight for survival is their passion and it throws enough challenges at them every single day to negate the need for anything else to occupy their minds. You rarely see them golfing or gardening; you don't see them going for a walk or to the gym, and they don't go swimming or do yoga. I've never known a farmer do anything creative such as painting or pottery, or take a night class to study something new, or even just be passionate about reading. This is generally because they never have spare time to even think about exploring other avenues, they are completely occupied by farming and it sets them firmly in their ways. I have respect for people who do things for no other reason than wanting to do them. This is something I could never do. If there is no logic in something, then it doesn't sit well with me. I wish I could mindlessly enjoy myself and let go, but I can't. This is what farm life does to people. It moulds a person into what the role demands, making it hard for farmers to fit in anywhere else. Nobody likes feeling awkward or feeling they don't fit in, it's a horrible place to be, but it's how a work burdened farmer feels whenever they are forced into social situations, especially those involving townsfolk.

Parties and Christmas can be horrific. Pass-the-parcel is torture to a farmer and having to wear paper hats and pull crackers can take them to the brink of destruction. As soon as the opportunity arises, they will flee the scene with all the speed of a bird that has accidentally flown inside a house and needs to beat a hasty retreat. They will return to their natural environment, their comfort zone, and breathe a sigh of relief. People sometimes try to involve farmers in social events, taking them under their wing as if they are in desperate need of help to make friends. They don't understand. The farmer doesn't need to be pitied in this way. Farmers can be the hardest of the hard, they're realists, and they've often had more than their fair share of misery. They're not looking to be taken under anyone's wing, they're simply too hardened to frolic with unnecessary acquaintances.

For young people, joining a Young Farmers Club is the best way to ensure social gatherings can be enjoyed with like-minded people. Any non-farmers who join are there because they want to learn about farming, so the great divide is already bridged. People that have been Club members often remain friends throughout life because they share a way of life and there can be no misunderstandings about the farming life. I never went to the Young Farmers, but I now regret it. I never made farmer friends when I was young, and the friends I made outside of farming were living in a different dimension, so the friendships never lasted. These days I'm too hardened by farming life to make friends, those times have passed me by.

A farmer's hostile attitude is a means of protection against nuisance people. In my youth, I was on the receiving end of this hostility many times. New employees arriving on a farm would often be subjected to the same treatment, a form of deliberate hostility to instil some sort of discipline. I'd be looked up and down and asked, "Can you do the job?" or, "Are you any good?" I was disgusted by the bluntness and hard-knock style of management that left the impression of a prison guard dressing down the prisoners. The belittling made my blood boil, but I've come to realise that they were protecting themselves from the inevitable no-shows the next morning. I was never a no-show and always earned the farmer's approval in the end, no matter how much of a miserable b*gger they were. I may have come to understand the reasons for their hostility, but looking back, it was unpleasant, and I feel bitter that I had to put up with so much of it.

The Lonely Thoughts of a Farmer

Working alone can be thought-provoking, it is not the same as just being alone. The difference is that the mind is in working mode, the lack of distractions lets it sink deep in. A slow relaxing pace can intensify meditation. A good example of this is when a farmer is working the fields on a tractor. This is different from being on the roads. When using machinery that is powered by the tractor, the engine is set at a constant throttle. The monotonous buzz makes the tractor into a kind of bubble where nothing else can be heard. The powerful vibrations run through the body and the driver is locked in a solitary isolated space, thoughts will swim around the head all day until the tractor is switched off and then the mind will be then released back to earth.

The field that the tractor works in will have been there since anyone can remember, before cultivation, it would have been as nature intended. These fields often overlook towns, cities, roads and motorways. Working the unchanged fields for a lifetime, a farmer will have watched the landscape slowly change. Buildings that stood throughout the childhood of their grandparents will disappear and be replaced with something different. The once bellowing smokestacks will have vanished, and the shiny glinting glass of new buildings will have replaced them. Electric generating windmills have recently sprouted up and increased traffic can be seen. The road haulage is constantly evolving, watching it is an insight into what is happening around the country, some cargo can be seen in the open air on the flatbed trucks. The advertisements on the side of lorries keep up to date with the demand, the ways of the masses and the politics of the times.

The timeless farming of the fields is in a comparative time warp, watching the world go by, it can create a feeling of longevity, watching everything come and go around you, it feels like you are the only constant thing around. Where does all the passing traffic come from? and where does it go to? All this contemplation works its way around to one's own mortality. Nobody can avoid change indefinitely and old mother time has her ways of dropping her hints to the farmer.

There are many bits of agricultural equipment which the farmer only sees for a short time each year whilst it is being used, this relates to the seasons. The hay baler, for example, it comes out from under the tarpaulin where it was put to protect it from the weather during the autumn, winter and spring. Uncovered, it looks exactly the same as when it went under one year ago. But the flesh and blood that works alongside of it is noticeably one year older. Many farms have an old tractor, the type that stayed and never needed upgrading or changing. No replacement could have done its work any better and the old tractor would be simple to maintain and repair. Such tractors have seen young farm lads turn into grandfathers. The seemingly immortal metal makes the farmer think how their own grandfather drove it all those years ago and how it will ride on long after their own death.

The seed drill and the fertilizer spreader alike weather well, a month to them is like a decade to the flesh. The livestock has a similar effect on the mind, seeing the breeding stock turn from being young and fertile into old and worn out. The memory of all the faithful companion dogs who have come and gone and the mud stains that they have left behind in the tractors and on the wallpapers in the kitchen. These comparisons and thoughts amongst many others make the farmer think how their mortal time is slowly dwindling.

There are references all around us that tell us exactly what the time of year it is, for those of us who work with the seasons, these events are special and quite sensational. For example, after a long brutal and toiling winter where the water pipes have been frozen up and the snow has lingered on the ground. Such winters can drag the farmer down, when everything requires twice as much effort and takes twice the time. A kind of depression can set in, it slowly accumulates until the farmer forgets that the winter will ever come to an end. Feelings are at their lowest when surprise strikes, almost like a last-minute reprieve. The first signs of spring magically appear and there is bird song, the subdued farmers spirit will awaken along with the daffodils, the colours of spring is a rebirth of another year and the warmth makes the farmer feel twenty years younger. Such moments are significant to the farmer, people who are not affected by the weather may pay little or no attention whatsoever to these kinds of seasonal change. A Farmer will stare at a winter sky with frost on the ground and amaze at the moving clouds as they change colour and the sound that the wind makes in the low air pressure and damp. The comparison with that of the hard-working summer is fascinating, they are poles apart, the farm endures them in sequence repeatedly. It brings thoughts of how the high temperature, air pressure and warm breezes are needed to harvest the grains in the summer, so essential to survive the winter. The crackling coal fire in the kitchen is a necessity during the biting winter months, watching the fire when the nights have drawn in dark by five in the evening. The memory of sweating uncomfortably in summer with no heating and only wearing shorts and a t-shirt is almost confusing. The mind wonders at the world turning on its axis whilst travelling around the sun, from there the mind wonders onto the origins of the universe. It is not hard to understand why farming families used to be so religious, they were at the mercy of skies.

I think that this is what instils the rare quality of being humble into the old-fashioned farmer types. As I have mentioned previously, I write about the real-life gritty farmers. The ones which had dirty old clothes and who had to fight to make a living. Even when times were good, they were always aware of how things could rapidly change. There are never two years alike when it comes to the weather, early and late rains and frosts can dictate the whole farming year, overly dry summers, heavy rain and freak winds can ruin crops. Disease can jump out of nowhere to sweep through livestock and devastate. An older farmer will have seen it all in their time and will greatly appreciate when things are running smoothly. I wonder if this knowledge and foresight are what makes the stereotypical farmer so tight with their money, always saving for poorer time ahead. There is sense in this, but seemingly not popular in these modern times. The old philosophy that 'you can not spend what you don't have' doesn't seem to stick anymore, a farmer will frustrate at the nation's rising debt. Farmer types get the impression that too many people vote mindlessly for increased public spending with no notion of where the money might come from or how the debt will be paid off. Some people might think that tax should be continually increased on businesses, however, those who have never tried running a business don't always realize how difficult it is. Business can be fragile, those without the experience often talk as though they are bottomless pits of money.

A self-employed farmer must make sure that their business is sustainable, otherwise, it will fail. It is hard to make do and mend and avoid luxuries all the time. However, a true farmer takes pleasure in keeping things simple, they will have learned from the first-hand experience that saving money is easier than making it. Money can easily be spent and borrowed, any idiot can do that, the creation and maintenance of wealth it is an entirely different matter. The farmers who survive will have seen many that have failed and be wise to the reasons why. Many farmers sons have learnt a hard lesson when they have been given the reigns of the cheque book. The yields of their wise old father's ways can often give a false sense of security to the sons who think that business comes naturally and that they cannot go wrong with farming. The silent wisdom of thrift knows what the finances of the farm can and cannot sustain. I have seen young bold farm lads buy new tractors, land rovers and other equipment in a blaze of glory, buying up or renting land at an astronomical pace. They have almost always failed when trying to go big fast. It can be an unfortunate lesson that can be avoided with a little thought. Why did the old wise farther never buy a hundred-thousand-pound tractor or build a five-hectare cow barn? It was because he knew that it wasn't warranted and that the same profit could be achieved by just plodding along, it is a mistake to work more for less just for the sake of it, but many young upstarts do. If they survive the long painful financial road back to where they were in the first place, they are wiser and weaker from the experience.

In conflict to this, I once knew a farmer, he was not from a farming family but he succeeded on an industrial scale, he borrowed lots of money to buy land, he invested in machinery and employed many people, it was a rare success story. Across the way from him was an old humble family farmstead which seemed to annoy him, they were quiet and humble, they kept themselves to themselves. They sustainably worked their farm and they were content. One day they popped up in conversation and the successful farmer who I knew said with a tone of envy in his voice 'they will be there long after we have gone' and he was right. The mega farm went to great heights, but the worth of the place caused tension between the siblings and it finished. The old humble farm across the way carried on regardless, it was not driven by money, this was a priceless thing.

Such careful farmers are often misunderstood and stand alone. They themselves will endeavor to think about other people's ideologies and often be confused by them. They generally hold to the opinion that people who vote for big spending governments are short-sighted and that anyone aiming for a sustainable existence should be more conservative with money. Farmers have traditionally passed their business down to the next generation so that they can carry on working them for a living, they act only as custodians until their children take it over. The farmer will muse at some of the City folks who vote for pay rises, more holidays, reduced bills and better working conditions. Some would just milk their employer into the ground, many will spend all their money and then borrow more to spend on luxuries, this behavior doesn't add up to the farmer, but it will often continue until disaster strikes. More pension money is desired, yet an earlier retirement age is requested at the same time, these things contradict each other at a basic level. There can be a complete lack of willingness to compromise. Some people have never seen bad times and are ignorant of them, they do not seem to understand how poorer times could be just around the corner. There have been various cases of large business losing money whilst at the same time their employees have campaigned for pay increases, they predictably went bust, then the complaint was being unemployed. The farmers common sense bluntness would ask the question that if someone thought that they were worth more money than what they were getting paid, then why didn't they prove it by going to get it somewhere else, by going self-employed for example. This would be a rhetorical question from the farmer, implying that they would have already done so if they were capable. Farming is essentially a basic type of business, this is why many farmers have such hard-line basic views, they cannot easily understand how institutions can function when they have no product to sell and think that their finance must come from leaning on others. Businesses must make their finances work, this is why farmers cannot understand things that do not add up. Some people live for today and say it is up to the next generation to sort themselves out. Is that selfish? It's a bit like old age pensioners saying that they are spending the kid's inheritance. Does this mean that they care more about themselves than they do their kids? It is anyone's prerogative I suppose. Spending every bit of excess on yourself seems selfish to me, if farmers did that, there would be no farms left.

Politics is complicated, not everybody can be pleased all at the same time and people's mindsets can be completely different. People can look at each other in disbelief and sometimes never understand the other's point of view. It all comes down to an individual's outlook, it isn't hard to understand why it is best not to discuss politics with friends.

The old type farmer tends to have basic common-sense views. They cannot make sense of the new world which has raced far ahead of them. A farmer may think that the simple little things of the day are too often overthought by 'over the top' delegates until something ridiculous always wins the argument. Farmers are in a minority in many ways and they know it. They tend not to bring attention to their way of life if they can help it because they know there are so many misconceptions and misunderstandings around it. Visits to the dentist, hairdressers or doctor's surgery can often yield friendly but inquisitive questions from those of a different dimension. Have you got the day off today? Or what are you doing this weekend? such questions do not compute with farmers and it can rapidly snowball into the complete opposite of opinions and politics. Once rumbled, the farmer is automatically assumed to be a millionaire and often asked, 'why don't you sell up and go on a cruise'? The asker of the question will be unable to comprehend any reason why not to sell out and blow the proceeds, that's what they would do in an instant. The farmer will be thinking that they would rather sell their soul when hell freezes over. The hard farming life yields the substance to be strong and carry on, where would a farmer move to if their farm was sold? A cruise would make a hard face farmer feel like a sissy and such a lavish holiday would feel self-indulgent and weak. Not many people could ever understand this. To avoid this type of confusion, I often used to tell people that I was going golfing on the weekend, something that they could understand, and which would not provoke any further questions. I would say that I had the day off work because it was my birthday and that I worked for the council. Bland but content responses would peruse, things like 'that's nice'. I often thought that members of the traveler community probably did the same thing as me, it is much easier to tell a little white lie rather than reveal what you are, that being something that can not be understood.

After trips into the town and the altercations with people from the great indoors, the farmer type will return home with an overwhelming feeling of home sweet home. He or she will reflect on their day and think about how lucky they are to have the life that they have. They do not always realize that they have been tailor-made to slot in right where they are, therefore, they do not fit in anywhere else. They will try to imagine an urban existence, but they can only concede how awful it must be. It is the same for everybody alike, comfort is found in things that are familiar, unfamiliar things can be frightening.

The Country Mouse Goes to Work in the Town

I was a farm boy born and bred, but I needed a change. The farm world was wearing me down, so I took a job in the city. Farming was not just physically hard work, it was mentally draining having to deal with all the oddball characters that floated about in the countryside. For a thinking man like myself, it was time to try something new before farming life pushed me over the edge. My new life brought some delights, but there were also new obstacles and disappointments to face.

I started work in a large utility company. It was a rota of four days on and four days off, and I had 30 days paid annual leave. It was ideal. I was earning a full-time salary and I had more time to spend on the farm at home. I was overjoyed not to be working on other people's farms anymore, and I felt smug that I'd left their problem staff behind.

The utility company was like a new world to me. It took me all over the place, and to places I'd never have visited if I hadn't been in the job. I saw towns, cities, villages, and areas all along the coast, and it was different every day. It taught me a lot about myself and made me realise how different the farm scene was. More importantly, it cleared some mist for me, showing me how my life experiences had made me different from the masses. The job was easy with no pressure, and no early starts or late finishes. I no longer had to worry about getting to bed super early, and in the mornings I'd get up at half six and do an hour or so of work on the farm and still have time to make a fry up before starting work at eight o'clock. Company work started when I turned on my laptop, and the company van was parked right outside my door. It felt like I was on holiday. The comparison between this job and my old job was absurd. All I had to do to begin my day's work was press a button, and I could do this when I was still at home. Previously, when I wasn't working at home for nothing, I'd have to get up at half three in the morning, rush a cup of tea with some biscuits for a bit of energy, get in my truck and travel at my own expense for half an hour, then get changed into overalls before using the clocking-in machine to start getting paid for my time. Sometimes, I'd need to fuel up at the all-night petrol station on the way to work, meaning I'd have spent my day's earnings before I'd even started.

My new job supplied a fuel card and the van. I never had to pay for transport again, so I sold my pickup truck. No more expensive garage bills, tax, MOT test or insurance for me, the company stood the lot – another burden lifted. My travel time was paid for, including to and from work, and there could be three or four hours spent travelling in a day. This, along with my lunch break, meant that my actual working time equated to around five hours per day. What a contrast. I struggled to come to terms with just how much of a miserable toil I'd endured before and how enjoyable and easy the new job was. In farm work, the farmers would go ballistic about the costs involved whenever anything went wrong. There would be blame to pin on someone which caused a terrible feeling of guilt, and it always made me feel that I had to be superhuman to ensure nothing would ever go wrong. At the utility company, nothing was ever anybody's fault. I found it hard to comprehend.

The Company had management in place to take care of things, it was organised. The chaos of trying to organise a rota with mentally challenged and unreliable colleagues quickly became a distant memory. If anyone was being antisocial or acting strangely, management would intervene, taking the individual away to deal with them in the appropriate department. It was bliss. I didn't have to humour unhinged workmates anymore, they could just be directed to occupational health. I could request days off as annual leave, and the requests were always accepted and covered without question. This was normal for everyone else, yet I couldn't believe how good it all was. I never fully came to terms with how little was expected of staff. The working conditions were excellent with good hours and good pay, but not everyone felt the same.

Most people hadn't suffered as I had, and they had no idea how good they had it. They were dissatisfied with their lot and complained about everything. Common sense and life experience were widely absent, and it seemed the Unions won pay increases every year for the sake of it. It struck me that some people thought they should get a full salary for doing nothing at all, and I used to think to myself that they should try being self-employed. If they were, I doubt many of them could earn fifty quid in a week. Ignorance is bliss, and the ones who complained most had no idea how lucky they were to have such a cushy job. They also had no idea how useless they were. As far as I was concerned, it was a luxury job. It kept me warm, clean, and dry, paid me a good salary with holiday pay and a pension, and even supplied a decent uniform. It was a far cry from being cold, wet, barely paid, and splattered with cow sh*t.

Many other good things came with the new job. When I was working in towns or cities, I noticed that people rarely bothered each other with pointless conversations or questions, unlike in the country. They minded their own business and tended not to be nosey. This must be urban wisdom, and I liked it. Nobody came and asked me what I was doing when I was working. I'm sure they can't have known what I was doing, but they didn't care. It was great not to be hassled. A lot is constantly going on in a busy town and people are rushing about their business, so there's no time to make small talk or to pester workmen, and they'd just walk past as though I was invisible. It's understood that there's no need to say hello to each other, there are just too many people about, so it's not considered rude or awkward. It made me smile to think about how often I worked in fear and trepidation in the countryside where passers-by had a habit of constantly interfering or making a nuisance of themselves.

The townsfolk I worked with had social skills. They knew where the boundaries were, and it was easy to work with them. I didn't know these people, but I could happily work with them without getting over-involved. It was pleasant and civil, and people tended to have a work-life and a home life that they kept separate, unlike in the countryside where it all gets mixed into one. I never arrived home from work to find one of my colleagues waiting for me, as Bernard did. However, I was still scarred from the rough of farm life, and I'd become cold and bitter. This wasn't an obstacle at work, provided I was polite and courteous to everyone, nothing else was anyone else's business. They knew I was different, but they could never quite put their finger on what it was. How could they? They were townsfolk and they wouldn't know such farmer-type ways, or how they had developed. It mattered not, and I was accepted just as everyone else was without prejudice. Sexism or racism could be sackable offences, I loved it. There were values and behaviours in place that were to be adhered to and I liked it so much because it created a barrier that would keep unsuitable people out. My previous farmworker colleagues would never pass the interview to get in, and then there were the mandatory courses that everyone had to complete, including one on micro-behaviours that pointed out how offense could be taken indirectly from something that had been said, or how even throwaway comments could cause upset. Derogatory comments about anyone's appearance were totally unacceptable, and I wondered how this course would go down with the farm brigade if they had to do it.

I fitted in perfectly with these values. I was efficient and soon became recognised as a hard worker, and when I was given work, everyone knew it would be done and all the loose ends would be tied up. My stumbling block was the social banter. There were lots of offices and I sometimes had to work in them. Regular meetings were held, but quite often the whole drawn-out thing was nothing but social banter. I felt like a fish out of water. I don't think this was visible to anyone else, and if they'd known, they'd have tried to help me with the way I felt. My self-sufficient ways would never have allowed me to even contemplate asking for help with something so personal, and I'd never known or experienced such high standards of welfare, in fact, I'd never before experienced any welfare at all.

Office desks are often personalised with photographs and objects, things that have a meaning, usually emotional or sentimental. I didn't get it. It all seemed a bit too soft for my liking, either that or it was something I just didn't understand. Supporting a football team was something else that almost felt mandatory, and there were mascots and stickers all over the place. I had no time for it whatsoever and I was disturbed by how seriously it was taken. To me, football seemed to be a substitute for something that was missing, and it struck me that these easy lifestyles lacked drive and practical accomplishment. Perhaps watching football filled the gap and provided something like a chase for victory. I already had enough chasing to do on the farm, and I didn't need football to feel I'd accomplished something. To this day, I've never understood why football is included in the news headlines, but maybe it's just a reminder of my apparent differences. My desk had nothing on it other than a computer and a few pencils. I could walk through huge offices split into cubicles and see desk after desk adorned with personal items. I found it intimidating, feeling almost like an alien walking on an unknown planet. These people lived and worked indoors. The heating was always on, even in the middle of summer. The coats on the hooks looked expensive and fashionable. Image was very important in these places, and everyone came to work smartly dressed and with their hair sharply groomed. Tattoos were prevalent. I'd always thought of tattoos as a sign of being hard and rough, but these were different. They were stylish and often contained sentimental messages, and they were apparently the trend of the times. I couldn't help thinking that it was short-sighted to have a tattoo; things change but tattoos don't. These people did as they pleased, and I admired that as it was something I'd never done. I was always constrained by the weather and farming. These were people living for the moment at the cutting edge of modern times, unlike me. I thought about everything, and I made plans and contingency plans before doing anything.

There were hundreds of people in the office and being among them could make me feel lonely. I could fit in where work was concerned, but I'd never be understood by any of them. I reminded myself of Hannah Hauxwell, the old farming spinster who lived alone out in the Yorkshire Dales. She was exposed to the world through a TV documentary called "A Winter Too Many" that told her story. She and I had things in common, and I knew from watching the documentary that she was never very comfortable with modern people and their ways. Both she and I were old-fashioned; we were a bit too serious and sensible for modern times. She sold the farm and moved out when it became too much for her, but when leaving in the removal van, she famously said, "Wherever I go, whatever I do, this will always be me."

I used to avoid lunchtimes in the office like the plague. I'd say I was going out to buy my lunch, and when I got back, they'd still be seated in the communal areas, and they'd ask where my lunch was. I'd say I'd eaten it and head straight back to my desk. They were welcoming and they wanted me to join them, so I openly told them I was a social retard. I had learned from experience. I'd tried sitting with a bunch of them before, only to find the conversation was beyond me. It was all about sports – mainly football, cricket, and racing cars – and if it wasn't sport, it was pop stars. I knew nothing either way. Another hot topic was technology, and discussions would be about gaming systems, mobile phone technology, and every other kind of consumable they could spend their wages on. I wasn't used to the idea of buying things for fun, it was a foreign concept to me. The practical reasoning I'd developed told me that there was no use in any of it, and I couldn't even force myself into being interested.

I'd purchased a mobile phone before starting the new job, and I remember taking it out of my pocket to check a message one lunchtime, only to see startled faces watching me. The surprised looks turned to barely disguised amusement as tight-lipped mouths struggled to hold back laughter. All eyes were on my phone. It was as basic as they come with no frills or extras. Needless to say, they all had the latest all-singing-all-dancing phones, so my "prehistoric" model was a museum piece in their eyes. I saw what they were thinking and took it in good humour, tapping my phone on the desk and saying, "Very durable these phones, this should last me years." Everyone burst out laughing. It wasn't in any way hostile, more a friendly laughter of acceptance. Nobody really cared; why would they? These trivial things didn't matter in an intelligent environment.

I managed to cause hilarity on another occasion when the conversation turned to pop concerts. I tried to join in by saying I'd recently gone to see The Wurzels. This was met with shrieks of laughter. Not everyone in the room had even heard of the scrumpy band, but those who had wouldn't have gone to see them if they'd been playing for free down in the car park. Music was an important part of these people's lives, they could identify themselves and other people through it, so I did receive one or two looks that implied WTF, but I suppose it gave a little insight into my world. People couldn't believe I'd never heard of the megastars they all raved about, wondering where I'd been for the last 20 years. Someone once asked if I'd been doing time in prison. I laughed it off, but the comparison to someone who'd been locked away was a little too close to the bone. It made me wonder about things I'd missed out on, spending all my time just working. Had all the work and little play made me into a dull boy?

These lunch table conversations were mostly inconsequential. They never delved into anything of importance and no one was any wiser after they'd taken place. It was just talk for the sake of it, but this was the very thing I couldn't do. They all bounced off each other, responding to one another's statements without even thinking about it. It reminded me of the hens at home, contentedly clucking away in the hen hut. It was a relaxed atmosphere, but not for me. I couldn't gabble away like the rest of them and could never think of anything to say. They'd talk about their food, saying what they liked and what they disliked, and maybe tell the story of how they'd prepared it. I'd be racking my brain trying to think of some kind of response, but this was difficult when there really was nothing to say about it. This wasn't conversation as such, it was more a case of everyone just saying things out loud and not necessarily expecting any relevant response. It's what they did, and it was their way. It was mindless banter at break time, and I'd found there was no interest in talking about anything serious. Break time was break time and any discussion of work was unwanted. This must have been normal because it was the same in every office all over the North. It was the norm for all these different groups of people, so I knew that it was me that was the odd one out.

The regular meetings I had to attend were almost the same. I had to sit through hours and hours of meetings, sometimes with 20 or as many as 100 others, and they often yielded absolutely nothing. It could take up two or three hours of my day, and I'd leave having learned nothing new. I became known as "quiet", only speaking when there was something worthwhile to be said.

People would constantly take centre stage, repeating blindingly obvious things, yet they seemed to get credit for it and often got promoted. My common sense and seriousness held me back and left me unrecognised. I think to some, it perhaps looked like it was all above my head, but in fact, I was only confused over why these basic things were even being talked about – again. I had what it took to organise and manage, I'd done it as a kid, but climbing the ladder in this company wasn't happening for me. I watched with bemusement as happy go lucky, forgetful, and incompetent people sauntered into managerial positions. I saw big mistakes being made by management, mistakes that cost thousands and thousands of pounds. It's easy to say in hindsight, but they were mistakes I wouldn't have made. There was never any blame and no one was demoted, that's not the way they worked, and people continued to be put into management roles based on popularity, social skills and who they knew. It did annoy me that performance wasn't recognised, that's where I did well, but I had a communication barrier. It was the barrier between townspeople and country people that was holding me back. However, I still had a job that was ideal for me, and I still had my jobs on the farm, so I was happy enough. It was known that I couldn't engage in social banter, but it hadn't gone unnoticed that I had other skills. Whenever work was being planned on a farmer's property, I'd be pushed forward to sort it out by someone saying, "He can speak farmer talk."

I had more time to spend on the farm at home than I'd had before, but I still felt guilty when I wasn't there. I'd always had this feeling, even when I was working on other farms. There are always things that need doing on a farm and the weather or time of year would be a constant reminder of this. For example, on a dry day in early summer, I'd be thinking that I ought to be spraying weeds and that it'd be too late if wet weather should set in. Or in winter, I'd be worried about pipes freezing up and thinking about wanting to check on the livestock. The cows never seemed to calve on the correct date, they were always early or late, and it was a worry that I might not be there for the times when they needed assistance. Harvest time was the worst. If it was a hot summer day and the grass was cut but needed to be turned, it was torture being out on a job that could be miles away from home. The rare strength of summer sun should always be utilised as it can be a short window of opportunity. On the right day, the grass can be turned several times to dry it out, and as the saying goes, you have to make hay when the sun shines – it's not necessarily going to do it for long.

On a farm, unexpected jobs seem to arise from nowhere and any given day is subject to a sudden turn of events. There were often times when I'd find myself glad to have been at home when something happened, but it also made me worry about what might be happening in my absence. Trying to be in two places at once is not only uncomfortable, it's also impossible. During harvest time, there was always an element of panic, and it was a race to gather in the crops and fill up the barns and grain bins before the weather broke. Any spell of prolonged rain could put everything into short supply and lower the quality of the crops. On one hot afternoon, I found myself stuck in a painfully long meeting. It was perfect weather for baling straw and I was desperate to get out, but I had to sit there with the sun streaming through the office blinds. I kept looking at the clock and time seemed to be standing still. There are no words to describe how much I wanted to escape, and I even spoke up in the meeting to point out that we'd discussed the topic just the week previous – and the week before that. I was trying to move things on, but it didn't go down well. People must have wondered what was wrong with me, and I think most of them enjoyed wasting the afternoon away, seeing it as a wind-down before home time. It used to fascinate me to think that I was the only one in the room with this problem, everyone else would be leaving work and their time was then their own to do with as they pleased. It didn't matter to them whether it was snowing, raining, or baking sunshine, the only difference it would make would be in their clothing choice. The contrast between their lifestyle and my own was mind-boggling. They saw hot sunshine in June as a chance to get a tan and have a barbeque in the garden with some cold drinks, but I saw it as a gift from God that was sent to help reap in the harvest and prepare for the winter months.

Of course, I had no right to be critical of the others. They could do what they wanted. I was the one trying to live in two separate worlds. I could never leave the farming world behind; it was part of me, but It was a love-hate relationship. The country life had priceless aspects to it that could never be disregarded or left behind, but money had tipped the balance and drawn me temporarily into a place where I didn't belong. Juggling the farm with another job made me a virtual steam train, driven and forced on until it was impossible to stop. I could never relax; I had to be constantly alert. Working with townsfolk brought it home to me just how different farm life was compared to theirs. It made me feel like I belonged to a different species, like a hare living among rabbits.

It was what it was, and I was who I was. It was another bitter pill for me to swallow. It was nobody's fault, but it all contributed to the feeling of having an extra-large cross to carry. The farming world couldn't provide me with a decent living, yet it had cursed me with this obstacle that would limit my success anywhere else. I couldn't overcome it, and to add insult to injury, it gave me a horrible troubled feeling whenever I was away from the farm. It was as though the farm world didn't want me, and out of spite, it didn't want me to go anywhere else either. When I started my town job, I felt a slight backlash from the farming people I knew. When they saw me in my uniform and in the smart new van, they looked at me differently. It perhaps surprised them at first because they wouldn't have known that I had the ability to change career, my potential having been hidden away for years. I transformed before their eyes and slipped seamlessly into the new role, helping them realise that the capability had always been there, but they looked at me differently and talked to me in a way that suggested they didn't know me anymore. There was something wrong. Some thought that I'd selfishly sold out from the farming life into one they didn't know or understand. This wasn't true. I was still farming; I just wasn't prepared to keep living the dog rough farming life that others had before me. I was in no man's land for sure, and I would remain so until I retired. Retirement from the utility company meant I could be home on the farm for good. Retirement from farming will never happen and I'll be here until the day I die.

The Wonders of the Farming Year

This concludes my sour and negative memoirs.

However, I could just as easily have written a whole book about the joys found within farming and the countryside. The priceless trinkets that each month of the year brings are treasures that never lose their appeal. Each month is unique, and farming is fused with natures events, creating a sense of constant wonder.

January is a time of hibernation; the absence of hedgehogs, bats, bumblebees, and butterflies defines it. It's the blackest month, and it's cold. Frost and snow may linger, and it can be a time to plough up fields, getting them ready to sow seeds that will flourish in the spring. It's also the time to spread manure on the land in preparation for the silage and hay. The frost is an advantage, making the ground harder so it's easier for the tractor to grip. The robin redbreast sings and inquisitively makes visits to every farm activity.

February is the shortest month; a good harvest is followed by a cold, wet, and windy February. Indoor jobs are selected where possible, repairing things that will be needed in busier times. Livestock needs to be fed with corn, hay, and silage, but the cold days make long nights by the fire, keeping cosy and eating stout, warming meals all the easier to appreciate.

March winds blow, alternating from the Arctic and the Mediterranean, signalling that winter is coming to an end. If the soil is dry enough, it's the month to sow the seeds, hoping there are no more deep frosts to come. It's said that a dry March will fill the barns and cellars and bring much hay. It's a good time for hedge laying, the saplings pointed towards the sun. The cows begin calving, the sheep start lambing, and early flowers begin to show.

April can still see winter lingering. It's cloudy, but it can bring sunshine and showers, frost, and rainbows. It's a time for planting potatoes, the cuckoo starts to sing, and swallows begin to arrive. The lambing is finished, and cherry trees start to blossom.

May is the month when the crops grow, the time of year in which they benefit most of all from plentiful rain. Fruit flies and all manner of insects come back to life. The fertiliser is spread to grow the grass, and crops are sprayed with pesticides and herbicides. Walls are repaired and the grass is chain harrowed to induce growth, and the tulips and lilacs are in bloom.

June is when the powerful sun and blistering heat makes for successful haymaking. It's a busy time, with tractors buzzing everywhere. Sheep shearing takes place, usually into the warm dusk nights, the wool rolled up and packed into hessian bags. When the day's work is finally done, the noises of the long day continue to echo in the mind. The agricultural show season starts, and roses are in bloom.

July is a time to marvel at glorious sunshine, but it's said that rain on the 15th, St Swithin's Day, will bring rain for another 40 days to come. Lean lambs are taken to market, the others vaccinated against worms. The combines start to work through the barley fields, and wild lilies sprout up around the edges.

August is the month in which grains are harvested, and the gathered straw placed in barns. It's the middle of summer, and the livestock eat around the unmown edges of fields after silage has been taken off.

September turns the green leaves to gold, red, and brown, and any berries left unpicked are spoilt. Mornings can be grey and misty with a heavy dew. Ploughing resumes, and it's the daisies and red poppies turn to stand out on the roadsides.

October brings a return of the winds that begin to blow dying leaves off the trees. Cattle start to come back into sheds after roaming freely in fields all summer. They begin to feed on hay or silage as the temperature drops. Hedge cutting is done after the birds have left their nests, and winter wheat is drilled for the following year. Flocks of wild geese can be seen in the skies, arriving from further north.

November is a time for cattle to be shut indoors, the grass outdoors has lost its goodness and the weather sinks into bleakness. The trees are bare, their trunks exposed, and the wind howls through the branches. Corn is bought and sold, and it's the time for tup sales. There are few flowers at this time of year, and the swallows migrate south into warmer climates.

December brings the shortest day of the year. There can be opportunities to repair dry stone walls if the weather's not too bitter. Feeding livestock is a daily routine, working around the different animals housed up for winter. The beef cattle slowly grow on the corn, it has the goodness of the summer sunshine within it.

The wonders of the farming year serve to remind me that all the negative things I've written about have a flip side. I have at times been at risk of contradiction, and I've abundantly used the words "often" and "sometimes". This is because there are no constants. Everything varies and everyone is different. There are exceptions to every rule, and no two people are ever the same. Every farm and every farmer will be different. There are trends of behaviours among farmers, farm staff, and urbanites, but there's also a swathe of people that fall somewhere in between. There will be farmers who go rambling down footpaths or ride horses, and there will be those who are familiar with life in the city. By the same token, there will be townsfolk who know all about the countryside and have full knowledge of agriculture.

I seem to have experienced the extremes of people and very little middle ground. I came from what would become the last of the old-fashioned farm stock; we were trailing behind, and we were clinging onto a way of life that was no longer financially sustainable. The small family farms were dying out, mass production and conglomerates supplying supermarkets instead. Ironically, now that most of the small farms are gone, they appear to be coming back into favour. It's now a popular craze to get produce straight from a quaint little farm, whether it's milk, eggs, or vegetables, and the simple life that was wiped away by the machine of modern life is now a newfound novelty.

I was unfortunate. My gas-tight farmer employers were decades behind the times and the awkward, strange people I worked with belonged in a bygone era. I fell into a unique niche, a crack in time where these characters still existed, and the old world was struggling to work in parallel with modern times. The townspeople were too far removed from the old simple ways to appreciate country ways, and it caused problems. The old farm scene made me hard-faced and then it dwindled away, leaving me floundering between two worlds. I was cheated by fate.

I found comfort in midlife. I could live on the farm and work it for my therapy, and I had savings and pensions to support myself and my family. I found joy in watching my children grow up, and I wondered if they might want to farm as a hobby when they were older. Maybe things will change, and perhaps the small traditional farms will be able to make a decent living once again. If the kids were interested, I'd be there to protect them, and I'd use my bitter experiences to guide them away from the pitfalls I fell into.

fredlumb54@gmail.com
https://twitter.com/lumb_fred

Printed in Great Britain
by Amazon